So You Want to Be a Missionary?

Essential Considerations

By Don Mingo

Copyright © 2019 by Donald James Mingo, D. Min.

All rights reserved. No part of this publication may be reproduced, distributed or transmitted in any form or by any means, without prior written permission.

Mingo Coaching Group LLC
Cover Design by Daniel Mingo
Cover Photo by Ben White
Edited by Trinity McFadden
Proof editing by Kathy Mingo
Simon Dube Photo by Donald T Mingo

So You Want to Be a Missionary?: Essential Considerations

All Scriptures are from the New Living Translation unless otherwise noted.

ISBN 9781732352513

Dedication

To all missionaries past and present I dedicate this book. You are the unsung heroes of the church. Your sacrifices and dedication though often unacknowledged in this life will resound in the next.

Table of Contents

Paradise Lost 6

Paradise Regained 19

Know Before You Go 27

Killer Expectations 30

What's Moving You? 40

When You Get Hurt 45

Loneliness 69

Missionary Failure – The Lack of Good Soul-Care 74

Your Mission's Agency – Meeting the In-Laws 95

Tame Your Dragon First 102

Show Me the Money! 112

Language or Languish 126

Aim High But Aim Straight 136

Missionary Success - What is it? 148

Missionary Conflict - It's Not That Simple 156

Fruit Loops or Brand Flakes? 170

Missionary Transitions 176

When Your MK's Leave Home 193

When Your Brook Dries Up 202

Vicarious Trauma 208

Elijah's Cave 217

Leaving an Elisha Legacy 228

The Art of Leaving Well 235

"Q" 238

Reentry - Check Your Expectations 242
Well Done! 249

(1)

Paradise Lost

"The mind is its own place, and in itself can make a heaven of hell, a hell of heaven."

John Milton, *Paradise Lost*

In 1986, we—my wife, Kathy, and our three little boys—made final arrangements to depart for South Africa. At the very last church before our parting, we presented our calling to serve the Zulu people in South Africa. An elderly missionary approached me. Long retired from serving in the Congo, he said, "So you want to be a missionary?"

"Yes, we are ready to go!" I replied.

His next words sobered me quickly

Looking me straight in the eye, he challenged: "You don't have a clue what's coming. There are so many things you need to know before you go. I'll pray for you."

His words proved almost prophetic. He was right. After four years of Bible college and a two-year internship, I still didn't have a clue of the challenges awaiting us. I wasn't alone.

Tammy and Allen

The young missionary couple sat before me in complete distress. Only two years earlier, they shared their passion and calling for the Chaga people in Tanzania, Africa. Just 700 days before, their hearts beamed with confidence and excitement.

Now— back in the United States—the young couple sat broken, disillusioned, and bitter. What could possibly make such young, zealous, potential missionaries utterly barren?

Before leaving their family and friends for Tanzania, they both underwent four years of educational training. Allen met Tammy in his first year at college. Both were studying intercultural communication and ministry. They both quickly discovered they shared the same compassion for Africa. Marrying the next year, aspirations soared in expectation of their coming missionary service.

During a short-term mission's trip to Tanzania, they met many veteran missionaries. Tammy commented to Allen several times on the kindness and warmth in which the older, established missionaries received them.

Visiting the vast countryside, they were taken by the sincerity of the African people and by their singing and their love for God. Both agreed God was moving them to return as full-time missionaries. They felt particularly impressed with the Chaga people. There were so many opportunities to serve Christ. With their hearts knitted in purpose, they found their place to serve. They couldn't wait to return to the States, apply for missionary status with their church's missions agency, and begin raising financial support to fund their life and ministry needs.

Two years of fundraising brought the young couple to their "Send Off Sunday" at their home church. Elders laid hands on the couple, prayers were offered, and a send-off dinner marked the momentous day. Three days later, Allen and Tammy departed for Tanzania. From the moment they stepped off the plane onto the tarmac of their new home, "nothing worked out."

Now they sat broken in deep despair, experiencing a crisis of faith in God, the church, and themselves.

What happened?

Lisa

As a young, single missionary, Lisa participated in numerous short-term mission trips to Haiti with her Alabama church. This poor, third world existed just a few hours flight from her home. What caught her attention were the many needy orphan children on the impoverished island. As she helped care for needy Haitian children in feeding centers, orphanages, and schools an overwhelming sense of need consumed her.

Returning home, she applied for missionary service with the mission committee of her church. After six months of support-raising, she left for Haiti to join a team living in a mission compound that daily ventured out into Haitian communities. At first, she thought, "This is exactly what I was meant for!" But within six months Lisa returned to Alabama with a deep sense of shame that she'd failed her church, the children of Haiti, and herself.

What happened?

Jim and Sandy

During twenty years in New Zealand, Jim and Sandy tried just about every technique to plant a church. Initially—in their first few years—a small congregation developed. Momentum slowed, however, and the church died. Their prayer letters and ministry updates did not express their struggles and discouragements. When reporting to their supporters back home in the States, their words did not reflect reality.

They often returned home, and they raised additional financial support on every visit. Jim frequently commented on God's goodness in supplying their financial needs. But when they returned to New Zealand, Jim and Sandy soon slipped back into their missionary lifestyle of discouragement and depression.

Oh, they conducted a few Bible studies from time to time. When American supporters arrived to visit them, plenty of missionary activity occurred. After their guests left, the couple slumped back into their old lifestyle of visiting coffee shops and diners. Jim and Sandy lived like an old, retired couple, bored upon each day's awakening and seeking activity to stay busy.

What happened?

Don and Kathy

Don and Kathy served in the same town in South Africa for more than twenty years. The last five years of their ministry were marked by a striking change in Don's demeanor. Kathy noticed it. His sons realized something was wrong. The Zulu people with whom Don served noticed a problem, too. Concerned, South African friends approached Don. Then Dave—a South African missionary—asked for a meeting with Don.

Dave and his wife were born in South Africa. They were part of a group of five million white South Africans. His grandparents immigrated to South Africa from Europe in the early 1920s.

Dave was the director of a Christian retreat and a respected leader among the Zulu communities outside the town of Estcourt in KwaZulu Natal. Dave was greatly admired. Fluent in the language, he sounded like a native Zulu when he spoke. His work in the Zulu communities was almost unmatched.

Dave and his wife assisted poor black communities in establishing a variety of self-help, self-sustainable enterprises. From agricultural, textile, microlending, small business, clinics, schools, and so much more, Dave did it all.

His love for the Zulu people was apparent every time you were around him. His message of God's love to the suffering people in those poor villages and townships outside Estcourt was deeply appreciated by many.

During a visit to Greystone, David called out to Don in his South Africa accent: "Doan!" ("Don" often sounded like "Doan" when Afrikaners spoke.) He called out again, "Doan! Come over heeryah! We need to tawk!'" After making a cup of instant coffee, made acceptable with enough milk and sugar, the two sat down together. Dave's next words shattered Don.

With beaming blue eyes surrounded by his deeply wrinkled, sun-ravaged face, Dave began, "Doan, how long have you been in South Africa now?"

"Well, let's see, about eighteen years, I guess," Don replied.

"Yes, and you've done a particularly magnificent job my friend." Dave smiled.

"Well, thank you—I really appreciate that," Don replied, anticipating a warm conversation.

"Doan, there is just no other way to say it. You, my friend, are finished. You're done! At the end."

Taken totally off guard, Don replied, "Pardon?"

"Doan, look here," Dave continued. "You've done a brilliant job, but we're all watching you crash and burn now. My friend, you need to go back home to the States. We are concerned for you."

Don immediately pushed back. "Well, you've done this kind of work longer than me, so I mean…"

Dave responded: "Yes, but I am South African. This is my home. This is not your home, and you are not the same person I met those many years ago, when you first arrived."

Dipping a rusk into his coffee, he continued. "Don, you've hit the wall, my friend. We've watched you carefully—"

Don interjected roughly, "What do you mean 'we'? Who is *we*?"

Dave smiled. "You see, that's what I'm talking about, my friend. By 'we,' I mean your friends. We've discussed this, and I agreed to talk with you about your health and your family. You need to go back home. You are finished here. I've seen this kind of stuff with missionaries many times before. You've done better than most, but you are clearly at the end, my friend."

Don erupted. "Really? Really? Well, people underestimate me all the time! I'll make it." Leaving, he grunted at Dave, "Well, thanks for your opinion."

Five months later, Dave, who was a younger man than Don, died suddenly of a heart attack. This caught Don's attention. Within three years, Don and Kathy were pastoring a mid-sized church back in the United States. But the return "home" didn't help Don. Not at all.

The return "home" only exacerbated his mood. He wasn't any better there than in South Africa. In fact, his mood, attitude, and condition became worse. And, "home" didn't seem like home at all.

At the prompting of a pastor friend, he began seeing a Christian therapist who specialized in helping pastors and missionaries.

What happened?

Jim

Jim was a highly competent missionary candidate. After rigorous screening, training, and support-raising, Jim enrolled in language school in his field of service. But after three years of study, Jim believed God was not leading him toward a life of missionary service.

What happened?

Natalie

Natalie felt called by God to serve as a single woman assisting missionary couples in China. She fulfilled every requirement by her missions agency, raised her financial support, and left for China.

Upon arriving in China, Natalie's host missionary couple informed her that they had resigned their missionary commission and were returning home in six weeks. Just two months later, Natalie sat in her pastor's office back in the States feeling abandoned, betrayed, and alone. Several months later she resigned her missionary commission.

What happened?

Cyndi and Bill

Cyndi and Bill went to Mozambique with hearts full of dedication, love, and desire to serve God by working with the Makua people. Their ministry went well, and directors gave them high marks.

One horrible night, they were attacked, and things happened to them that shouldn't happen to anyone. Ravished and victimized, Cyndi and Bill took their three children back home to seek healing, recovery, and guidance. Nothing could give back what was taken from them; particularly Cyndi.

What happened?

Ted

As a single missionary, Ted went with the full support of his home church and missions board. God touched his soul to plant a church in the needy country of Belgium. As he learned the language, he met a young Belgium woman. They fell deeply in love and announced their wedding plans—but problems immediately followed.

Ted's fiancée was not mission trained or qualified. Ted's missions board refused to recognize her unless she went through the same lengthy training as Ted.

Their marriage ended Ted's time as a missionary. Returning to the States with his new bride, he left missionary ministry and the church. Today, Ted and his young bride live a secular life.

What happened?

Lenette

Lenette and her husband served in Lebanon as missionaries in the 1980s. One night while jogging, Jim slipped and fell down an embankment, striking his head. The fall killed him.

Kathy and I met Lenette in Kansas fifteen years later. She was living in a $200 per month mobile home, was in and out of relationships with men, and sporadically attended church. We spoke with her for quite a while. Daily life was a struggle for her.

What happened?

The McKenzie's

This couple entered missions later in life. Empty nesters, they raised their support in just eighteen months. Departing for South America, they left one of their sons at college in Texas.

During the second year of language study, their daughter gave birth to the first grandchild. Mrs. McKenzie began to crumble, sobbing, "I'm not ready for this. My heart is with my children. I want to see my grandchild."

After less than three years of service, the McKenzie's felt led by God to leave the field. They both work secular jobs, finding little time to participate in church much beyond attending a couple Sundays a month.

Their daughter and her husband moved due to a job transfer. The McKenzie's struggle to see their grandchild more than they once did as missionaries.

What happened?

Lisa and Dan

Lisa and Dan projected a wonderful image of a young couple totally sold out for the Lord. Their plan to enter a country in Europe and share Christ with secular twenty-somethings was met with wide enthusiasm.

In less than eighteen months they left for their mission field fully funded. This was no small feat for the expensive country of the Netherlands. But in less than three years they returned to the States.

They told their supporters that the Dutch government didn't allow homeschooling. Their only choice was to enroll their children in

North Holland's public-school system. In good conscience, they couldn't put their children in the public school.

Their missionary presentation of God's touching their souls to "reach the Hollanders" lasted less than three years.

What happened?

Gene and Cheri

In their ninth year of marriage Gene and Cheri arrived in their field. With their three children in tow, they began serving in an orphanage. Destitute children filled their rescue center.

With the demands of their ministry, they hired a young, local woman as a domestic servant to help with their children and household chores.

Back home in Ohio, Cheri's mom grew frail after fracturing her hip from a fall. Cheri flew back and forth for over a year to care for her mother. This left Gene with the work, the children, and the nanny.

After the death and funeral of Cheri's beloved mother, Gene served Cheri with divorce papers. It came out that during the many trips Cheri took to care for her mother, Gene made "love" with their domestic employee in the very bed Cheri and he had shared over their twelve years of marriage.

Gene abandoned his covenant vows to his wife to live with the house help. Their three children were left traumatized.

We don't need to ask, "What happened?", do we?

True Stories

I changed the names and faces here to protect the innocent. Adding substantial ambiguity puts the identification of any one individual mentioned beyond recognition.

Valuing missionary confidentiality, it is my purpose that not a single missionary can point to the above stories and cry, "Hey, he's talking about me." Rest assured, my promise of confidentiality does not waver. You are protected as some of the narratives blend with a touch of fiction to offer an added layer of defense.

The regularity of which such events occur assures that such stories find fibers of truth with many missionaries' tapestries of experience.

The story "Don and Kathy" is a slice of our personal history. That's an account of our struggles—*my* struggles—with post-traumatic stress disorder (PTSD) after years of serving in South Africa.

The purpose of this book is to encourage missionaries, pastors, and church leaders toward greater understanding of the stresses and pressures that exist for missionaries today. That is not to say times weren't tougher for missionaries of the past. But we live in the present. Right now. Today.

So You Want to Be a Missionary? Essential Considerations presents crucial contemplations for today's missionaries who face gauntlets of challenges in their missionary life and work.

There is growing resistance toward Christ, his gospel, and his message bearers around the world. National missionaries from third world countries to other impoverished countries share the same obstacles of persecution and discouragement. These obstacles are some of the most effective tools in the enemy's arsenal.

Our third world counterparts live on a fraction of the financial support American missionaries do. To say they bear some resentment at such inequity is an understatement. They are some of the most faithful, resilient, hardworking, and productive missionaries in the field today.

American missionaries carry three strikes against them from the very beginning. They are Americans. Strike one! Our recent military involvements in the Middle East and politics greatly reduce American friendly zones around the world. Much of the world doesn't like or want Americans in their countries.

> Half of all new missionaries do not last beyond their first term on the field.

They are also missionaries. Strike two! The term "missionary" is extremely pejorative. Fewer countries want career missionaries hanging around.

And they are Christian. Strike three!

These obstacles are not discussed enough in many mission circles with new missionary candidates. While learning theology, linguistics, and general ed courses, little if any preparation is offered in missionary survival.

Many western missionaries seem unprepared for the animosity that exists. Missionaries from other countries such as South Korea and the Philippians find far less resentment toward their nationalities and countries of origin.

Missionaries pose an undesired factor for governments today. Few countries want them. This is one of the many challenges facing missionaries today. Perhaps this is the reason that fifty percent of all new missionaries do not last beyond their first term on the mission field.[1]

So You Want to Be a Missionary? has only two goals. First, to honor and glorify God. Second, to encourage current and future missionaries to consider the many facets and challenges of their Christian missionary service. In this, a healthier you is the goal.

Missionary casualties often occur in a vacuum of poor self- and soul-care. Soul-care is rarely discussed. Many missionaries spoken with over the years struggle with dry, barren souls. Their initial vibrancy upon arriving on the field shriveled and died over their years of missionary service. In putting out, they gave and gave and gave until they ran out of any more soul to give.

> Missionary casualties often occur in a vacuum of poor self- and soul-care.

As one missionary shared: "This place was a paradise. I loved the people, church, and ministry. Now something's lost. I don't know what. It's not the same. I want to get out of here. I hate this place."

Does it surprise you to know that that missionary couple served only a few years in their paradise before it morphed into their personal hell? They returned to the United States spiritually debilitated, and they struggle to this day.

What happened?

(2)

Paradise Regained

"That who advances his glory, not their own,
them he himself to glory will advance."

John Milton, *Paradise Regained*

Missionary life is an extraordinarily rich experience with many rewards. It presents amazing opportunities to serve Christ in ways few other Christians can comprehend. It's also filled with steep learning curves that are necessary to gain a healthy perspective on missionary living.

A young missionary once expressed his views to a senior missionary, saying, "These people are so backwards. You can spend your whole life here and never find one that's trustworthy."

The next week, the older missionary invited the younger missionary to meet him at a local coffee shop. As the young missionary entered, he noticed three local men of color sitting with the older, white missionary. As the young missionary approached, all of them stood. The older missionary introduced the local black men as "my best friends."

Paradise or Purgatory

Decades ago, an old, Baptist, Swedish missionary in South Africa shared his predicament over a cup of Wimpy's[2] coffee. As a young missionary, I listened to the gaunt, elderly missionary lament his condition. He whimpered:

> "It's as if I wasted my entire life. I've worked endlessly, but this is all I have to show for it? My soul is finished!"

"Finished" is a common expression used in South African English to express "at one's complete end." His words, "My soul is finished," stuck with me. Jesus talked about such a condition. "And what do you benefit if you gain the whole world but lose your own soul?" (Mark 8:36).[3]

Idolizing him at that time, I posed a pensive question: "What was it you were trying to accomplish?" His list included many admirable ambitions and activities. What his answer did not include was any mention of the health of his soul. The very condition he mentioned earlier in our conversation.

The gracious, honored, old missionary slumped into a weak, discouraged, confused existence. It was a sad sad sight. He had gained much in ministry, much among his peers, much in his denomination, and much in accomplishments. Yet none of that satisfied. While doing all the churchy stuff, the crescendo of his final words impacted me deeply: "I came here to save souls, but I think I've lost mine." With that our conversation ended. I never saw him again.

Perspective Is Everything—Almost

Your view about others, success, failure, calling, and just about anything else will affect your missionary life and ministry. If you perceive the national people as ignorant, they're stupid. View them as greedy, they're thieves. See them as immoral, they're deviant. Consider them invasive, they're hiding something. See them as violent, they're murderers.

But if you see them as God's creation, they're beautiful. Perceive them as associates they're co-laborers. View them as knowledgeable about the culture, they become guides, tutors, and mentors. See them as souls for whom Christ died, they become highly valued. Attitude filters every thought process.

It's almost all in your perspective. Almost.

A missionary is a rare individual with the faith and courage to embark upon a life-altering course. There is nothing like it.

An image strikes me of an elderly missionary at a missionary reunion standing before a group of missionaries beaming with a huge smile. His words set a sweet bouquet for that week as he shared, "Missionary life is the greatest life in the world."

Bored or Bodacious

When speaking with millennials and post-millennials about missionary life, exciting, prompting words erupt from my soul:

> "If you want a life that's not boring, offers exciting adventure, endless avenues of learning, a great worldview, and brings people to Jesus in numbers you rarely see in the United States, consider missionary life! There is no other life like it!"

For those looking at retirement, I ask:

"Ever consider missionary work? Rather than spending your golden years wasting your few years left in trivial, boredom-breaking pursuits, become a missionary! Don't waste your life! Use those years of acquired skills and wisdom to advance God's kingdom rather than the buttons on your remote."

What's so great about the missionary life? Missionary life centers itself around what I like to call the 7 Fs of missionary life.

The 7 Fs of Missionary Life

Faith. Here's the thing: In missionary life, you'll experience living on faith's edge—a both exciting and terrifying place to live! Missionaries can experience Hebrews 11:6 at a rich, intoxicating level.

> And it is impossible to please God without faith. Anyone who wants to come to him must believe that God exists and that he rewards those who sincerely seek him.

Living on faith's edge is what I missed when I came off the field in 2006 after twenty-two years of missionary service in South Africa. It's what I now relish again after reentering missionary service in 2015. Witnessing the God of this universe reward us as we diligently seek him—there's nothing more exciting!

Selling our home and stepping out in faith with younger missionaries to raise support and live by faith again is exhilarating stuff! To know that God did a thing in answer to our prayers and needs and advanced this ministry beyond our ability to network is a rewarding faith walk few ever experience.

Raising monthly support presents daunting challenges. Several requests to speak at missionary retreats in other countries stood before us. The cost of the trips was above our financial means. After sharing our ministry—Missionary to Missionary Care—one Sunday, a woman walked up after the Sunday service and handed me a check. Later that afternoon we discovered the check was for five thousand dollars. This was enough to cover the costs of both trips for Kathy and me.

Freedom. Missionary life offers freedom and mobility that is found in few other professions. I loved being able to travel from Johannesburg, South Africa, fly to Minneapolis, Minnesota, and pick up a rental car and drive to my mom's house—all without a need for GPS!

Being able to go anywhere at almost any time offers something found in few existences. Missionaries often set their own schedules, travel where they desire, and invest themselves according to their own longings.

Finance. Many missionaries must raise finances to support themselves, their families and ministries. Support-raising, or "deputation" as it is called, is a tough task. These challenges provide upward opportunities for faith.

Good support-raisers often enjoy virtually tax-free existences. Housing sometimes is provided for free. You'll never get rich as a missionary, but many missionaries do all right. What one gains more than makes up for the sacrifices missionaries make.

Fame. Many in the church consider missionaries to be the heroes of the faith. In my opinion, this is true. I remember hearing Billy Graham once say, "Missionaries are the true heroes."

Many missionaries are cream-of-the-crop kind of people. They are at the upper echelon of Christian existence and calling. I suspect many churches treat missionaries better than they treat their own pastors.

Friendship. Missionaries make friends with people of different cultures. It's a highlight of missionary living.

While some missionaries cite having a lack of deep, long-term friendships, a missionary may experience multiple multiethnic relationships. While citing "loneliness" as a common grievance, healthy missionaries make friends in multiple countries.

Fervor. Although family and friends can't understand what propels a person to leave their home and place of birth, a missionary might answer, "Why would I stay?"

Many missionaries speak of an urge, confidence, moving, or touching of the soul to enter missionary service. Their callings are as unique as individual snowflakes that fall to the ground. Yet all bare one commonality: a touch from God.

Fulfillment. Missionaries understand the mandate of Christ's command to his church: "Go, make disciples of all nations." A sense of accomplishment, fulfillment, and life-change embeds itself in missionary service. Sharing God's love in practical ways with impoverished, hurting people gives one a sense of "making a difference." As one missionary shared, "There is nothing more strategic I can do with my life than become a missionary." His smile said the rest.

> "There is nothing more strategic I can do with my life than become a missionary."

For me—and many other missionaries agree—the missionary life is one of the most rewarding and exciting lifestyles out there. As another missionary put it: "Why contemplate doing anything else? Everything else falls short of this!"

Kate

Kate and her husband served in Uganda. They raised their three children there. After raising their children and after twenty-eight years of missionary service, Kate's husband died of cancer. Kate stayed in Uganda and served another sixteen years.

Her son stood with me in a church in Waukesha, Wisconsin, sharing this wonderful story of his mother, a woman I'd never met.

He said, "Mom has cancer now. After her latest treatment, she's going back to Uganda. She wishes to die in Africa with the people she's loved and served for almost forty years now. That's hard for me as her son, but I love her for it."

Kate kissed her adult children goodbye the next week. She died several months after returning to Uganda. The Ugandans laid her to rest next to "her people," having lived a full, rich, rewarding life. She wouldn't have changed a thing.

A life in missions work is—at least to me—like a paradise. The missionary paradise is starkly different from the first paradise mentioned in Genesis, I grant you that.

Our paradise—plush and beautiful—is a fallen one. In this garden, people need a way to return to their creator. In this garden, weeds, thorns, and thistles have overgrown many hearts. Wolves prowl among the sheep, too. Yet it is the place to which God has called me. It's a place where God meets me. It's the place God does his amazing work in and through me.

The missionary's garden provides pleasure—contentment and fulfillment—along with its many challenges. Garden cultivators must consider the condition of the soil. They must possess an understanding of the soul-life growing from that soil. And they must know how to deal with invasive pests seeking to destroy that garden. Understanding these challenges before entering the garden is the difference between success or failure.

This book is about considering those challenges—the encounters each missionary face—that determine whether gardening becomes a missionary's delight or a missionary's desolation.

Come along with me. Let this tattered, torn, old missionary share some thoughts.

And, my friend, they are only that. Put down your guard. Relax. Ponder. Use what you can. Discard that which you consider irrelevant.

And please forgive that with which you may take issue. My desire is to help you navigate the beautiful—yet stormy—waters you'll encounter once you leave your harbor to sail into open waters. I hope to help you experience both the beautiful sunrises in the safety of the harbor and the brutal waves in exposed seas that beat upon the hull.

It's in stormy waters—in the pounding waves—that the journey is secured. A voyage without the tempest is not worth the rigging of the ship, the raising of the sails, and the setting forth toward open waters. A ship only finds unhindered safety while sitting in the docks inside the harbor. Its truest purpose is discovered in thundery waters of service and ministry. It is here you discover both the wiles and the beauty of the deep.

Your soul requires much preparation to ensure its seaworthiness. Whether your vessel endures the many gales it will face depends on the many considerations you must know before you go.

(3)

Know Before You Go

"There is no greater evil than men's failure to consult and to consider."

Sophocles, *Antigone*

So You Want to be a Missionary? Essential Considerations is about missionary considerations, not dogmatic statements. There are no criticisms or judgements here. Sourced reflections from twenty-five years of missionary service and ten years in the American pastorate shapes my unique perspective. Considerations also arise from my exchanges with hundreds of missionaries currently and over the years.

This not a weighty theological or philosophical book on missiology. The aim here is to present practical thoughts to help you—the missionary—make good, solid choices in your missionary career. As such, my words bear a parallel to some of the

> Considerations offered here are meant to challenge, not pose dogmatic statements.

criticisms over the years that my preaching and teaching is too practical and not theologically weighty enough. This is a book of missionary practicality. About making it work. Making it work appears—at least to me—to be what's greatly lacking in missionary life and ministry today.

Prisms of emotions will show through the words that follow. Some passions reflect my love for the missionary life and calling. Other words share some harsh realities of missionary life. Many thoughts originate from other missionaries. As a young missionary shared with me just last night, "They never told us about any of this stuff." That stuff is the stuff talked about in the following pages.

My past missionary experiences bring a wealth of thought, life lessons, and perspectives for both new and current candidates considering a missionary life.

This book focuses on real-world, hands-on, everyday considerations. At the end of many chapters, considerations offered to you, the reader, hopefully will challenge you to think through your missionary steps.

Considerations offered here mean to challenge rather than state solitary, rigid options for your missionary life and work. My concern is for your health, missionary, and for the health of the thousands of missionaries who leave bright-eyed and bushy-tailed for the mission field, with unconsidered, staggering obstacles ahead of them.

And my heart leans heavily toward the multitudes of missionaries who return to their homes unwept, unhonored, and unsung.[4]

The following chapters offer considerations that will both resonate and challenge you. They also propose thoughts with which some will surely disagree—and perhaps even a few more that some may find irksome. Good.

This book is mostly about careful, considerate preparedness. If I could journey back into my younger years of missionary service with what I share in the following pages, oh, how much more prepared and effective I might be!

(4)

Killer Expectations

"Blessed is he who expects nothing,
for he shall never be disappointed."

Alexander Pope

Expectation is "a belief that someone will or should achieve something."[5]

It's a belief something should—or must—happen in a particular way and in a particular sequence, or that someone or something should possess a particular set of qualities or behaviors.[6]

> Expectations is the graveyard of many missionaries' callings and dreams.

Expectations probably result in more missionary casualties than any other single cause. Expectations is the graveyard of many missionaries' callings and dreams.

Expectational Killers

As I sat with a young missionary team in Africa, they shared their despair.

The entire young team came from the same wonderful church. All the team members grew up in their home church. Several years went into planning, fundraising, and team building. Before all the team members arrived on the field, their home church suffered a devastating split. This resulted in half the congregation leaving to start their own church. Before the last team member arrived on the field, the missionary team split, too.

Team members siding with the dissenting group leaving the church packed their bags and returned to the States. The remaining team members were overwhelmed. One young missionary stated, "It wasn't supposed to be like this." My reply was, "What was it supposed to be like?" The conversation continued for many hours over several days.

The dream of one complete, harmonious team of five couples from their home church to live and serve the beautiful people of this unique African country had changed irrevocably. Fortunately, this team enjoyed solid love and support from their church, pastors, and staff.

After regrouping and surviving their disappointment, three couples returned to Tanzania, where they serve today. But many such stories do not end this well.

A common statement rehearsed repeatedly by discouraged missionaries coming off the field is, "It was nothing like we thought it would be." The top expectational disappointments shared with me are:

- It wasn't at all what I thought it would be like.
- I was never so lonely.
- Nothing was the same as the short-term missions trips I took.
- My housing wasn't adequate.
- There was so much violence in the country.
- The veteran missionaries were impossible to work with.
- I wasn't sure what my responsibilities were.
- The veteran missionary was a workaholic and expected the same from me.
- My relationships with the missionaries who invited us to join them are not the same now.
- I'm just a workhorse for the older missionaries.
- As soon as we arrived, the veteran missionary took a furlough, leaving us in charge of everything.
- The local people didn't appreciate me.
- Our home church forgot about us.
- Our home church got a new pastor.
- Our home church suffered a split.
- Our sending agency forgot about us.
- The missionaries couldn't get along.
- God called us, but nothing was happening to advance the ministry here. We were going nowhere.
- I failed. Plain and simple.
- It was boring. There was nothing to do.
- Financially, we couldn't make it.
- The people over there were horrible. They lie, cheat, and steal.
- We didn't feel safe.
- My spouse didn't like the people, place, or preparation.
- I didn't feel valued.
- Other missionaries ignored me.

- The team I was on was toxic.
- No one listened to me. It was like, "You're new here. In five or six years, maybe you'll have an opinion we'll want to listen to."
- It was way different from what I thought it was going to be. *Way different*!

The Problem with Expectations

Expectation defines not so much what missionary life looks like, but rather what **it *must* look like**. Think about it for just a moment. Couldn't an expectation be perhaps considered as an idol? Yes, you know, one of those Old Testament handmade objects that the people of antiquity created with their own hands in their own image and then bowed down and worshipped. In this, an expectation develops into the missionary's idol when thought changes into "**the way it must be.**"

> Expectations can become the missionary's idol.

Check Your Expectations

Describe your expectations. Write them down. Go ahead. Give it a try. I dare you.

Start with, "This is what I want my missionary life and ministry to look like once I arrive on the field."

Then a new category: "This is what my missionary life and ministry must look like."

Maybe, you'll need a little help. Here is a made-up example that's exaggeratively accurate, I think.

A Missionary Prayer of Expectation

Dear God, when I get to the field, please get me the accommodations my heart desires. You know, that one with a front yard, in that neighborhood I really like, with the big picture windows.

Oh, God, please make the other missionaries become subservient to my hopes for my missionary success.

God, you said in your Word, "We have not because we ask not." Therefore, I ask that you fulfill my expectations, because Jesus said that if we have even a little faith we can move mountains. My expectation is that mountain. Make it so, Lord.

And you've placed deep in my heart a vision for the work. I know what's best for me and my ministry. So, make it so. Amen.

One more thing, God. Prepare the national people whom I will lead in your ways. You know, so that they do what I know you want them to do through me.

Oh, and if it doesn't work out, I will be very disappointed.

Here I come!

Amen.

Examine Your Expectations

I love the words of Milton in *Paradise Regained*:

> Much of the Soul they talk, but all awry;
> And in themselves seek virtue; and to themselves
> All glory arrogate, to God give none

I think—I know it was true for me—that much of our missionary work becomes too much about us, and not about *him*.

Where do your expectations originate? Please, think about that question. Where do notions of what your missionary experience should—*must*—look like—arise?

Perhaps your outlook demands trying to impose your desires upon God, or maybe upon yourself, but most likely upon the very people you're called to serve. Is it possible your expectations are based upon all others becoming subservient to your will?[7]

> Where do your expectations originate?

My Zulu pastors in South Africa often formed their English words from their Zulu grammar. When speaking English, they used to say during our vision meetings, **"Let's not visionate what God is not visionating for us."** These are good words. Don't visionate that which God is not preparing for you.

When we build missions strategies around our expectations, expectations become the fulcrum upon which we conduct God's business. We think that God must comply with our desires and people must conform to our way of thinking. It's a far cry from the apostle Paul's words, "Yes, I try to find common ground with everyone, doing everything I can to save some"(1 Corinthians 9:22).

What if we defined heaven by such expectations? And what if heaven turned out to be exactly the way one anticipated it to look and feel like?

Now contrast that with, "That is what the Scriptures mean when they say, 'No eye has seen, no ear has heard, and no mind has imagined what God has prepared for those who love him'" (1 Corinthians 2:9). Do you really want your expectations to come true rather than God's plans for your life and ministry?

One of the most fascinating aspects about missionary life is that we don't have it all figured out. It requires living on the front lines of faith, trusting God to meet our needs while he guides us in our God-ventures. Journeys and new experiences add variety to an amazing, unique lifestyle that few ever experience.

Expectations can squelch faith big-time!

Realistic Anticipations

Perhaps reshaping our desires, goals, and aspirations into a lesser, minutely definitive view is more helpful. From my experience—and from speaking with hundreds of missionaries—very little of your first few years will match your initial expectations. How could they? Most first-time missionaries possess little experience of living in another country and working with other missionaries.

Question: How realistic can one's expectations be before one learns the language of a people group, their culture, and their country? Your expectations become very ethnocentric when they're developed and birthed solely through the lenses of their own birth cultures. Expectations

> How realistic can one's expectation be before one learns the language of a people group, their culture, and their country?

birthed in the vacuum of an anticipated experience in another culture will always disappoint.

As one missionary director in Central America shared with me, "I see new missionaries' expectations dashed in seconds after they arrive on the field. They often leave the field and return to the States in bitter disappointment because as one missionary shared, 'It wasn't the way I thought it was going to be.' Usually their reasoning places heavy blame on everyone else."

Expectancy Better Aids Missionaries

"Expectancy" is closely related to "expectations." Expectancy can be defined as an "anticipatory belief or desire."[8] Think of it as an expectation without high demand or strict definition.[9] James, the half-brother of Jesus, dealt with this very issue. He wrote:

> Look here, you who say, 'Today or tomorrow we are going to a certain town and will stay there a year. We will do business there and make a profit.' How do you know what your life will be like tomorrow? Your life is like the morning fog—it's here a little while, then it's gone. **What you ought to say is, "If the Lord wants us to, we will live and do this or that."** (James 4:13-15, emphasis added).

Explorers anticipate an adventure not by defining the destination before they arrive. Their expectation is in the expectancy of the journey. Rather, they discover it. There is nothing wrong with anticipating or expecting a rich and rewarding experience. Forming your expectations around an attitude of adventure rather

> "What you ought to say is, 'If the Lord wants us to, we will live and do this or that.'"

than a preconceived perception of inevitability may greatly aid you in entering your new culture and way of life.

Expectancy That Rests in God

A Scripture I've grown to cherish is Proverbs 3:5-6:

Trust in the Lord with all your heart;
   do not depend on your own understanding.
Seek his will in all you do,
   and **he will show you which path to take** (emphasis added).

What if—just what if—one leaned not so much upon one's own "this is what I expected it to look like"? What if we learned instead to pursue God's expectations in every facet of our missionary lives and endeavors?

Expectancy sourced in God finds a surer footing than expectations adrift in self-centered aspirations. Let your expectancies become God's leadings into new adventures and discoveries.

Considerations

1. What expectations—or demands—lie deep within your soul? You know what I mean. Like the thoughts of, "When I get to the mission field, it will look like or must be like _____."

2. How can your expectations become realistic?

3. What are your thoughts about James's words, "If the Lord wants us to, we will live and do this or that," in relationship to your missionary calling?

4. Proverbs 3:5-6: Get hold of it. What insights can you dig out of this vast vein of truth?

(5)

What's Moving You?

> "Missionaries are very human folks, just doing what they are asked. Simply a bunch of nobodies trying to exalt Somebody."
>
> Jim Elliot, *Shadow of the Almighty*

What exactly are your reasons for becoming a missionary—which involves selling your house and goods and moving your family halfway around the world to begin a new life in a different culture, climate, and atmosphere? What moves you to do such a thing?

We're not going to debate what constitutes a legitimate missionary calling. That's been done, continues, and will not cease.

I find it interesting that in the vast universe of a creator God who placed the stars in the cosmos, created us in his image, and painted sunsets on canvases exploding with vibrant colors, that some hold a very narrow, definitive view of what constitutes a missionary calling.

The Tapestry of a Missionary Calling

The pendulum seems to swing somewhere between two views of a missionary calling: either the command of Jesus in Matthew 28:18-20 makes everyone a missionary; or only those receiving a definitive, direct moving of God's spirit for missionary service are called to it.

One follows the reasoning of the great, early pioneer missionary to China, Hudson Taylor:

> It will not do to say that you have no special call to go to China. With these facts before you and with the command of the Lord Jesus to go and preach the gospel to every creature, you need rather to ascertain whether you have a special call to stay at home.[10]

Bob Hughes, a missionary who served in the Philippians many years until cancer ushered him into the presence of God, argued, "Why do you need a call when God gave you a command?" I still remember hearing those words spoken in chapel more than forty years ago.

Many missionaries share a more mystical view of their missionary calling. One said, "It was during a missionary conference something happened. As a missionary from Ethiopia shared their ministry, I just knew. God called me to serve in Africa. That was twenty-four years ago."

This view shared by numerous missionaries appears less definitive, leaning towards a special touch, call, or impression. One shared, "You might say that my dissatisfaction with life as it was, and a desire to do that which God designed my soul to do, made my heart sing. That was God's calling for me."

Another missionary talked more about vision. She said, "While studying intercultural communications and missiology at university, I sensed a huge vision for what might be done for God's kingdom in another culture. I prayed, 'God, I am willing, please lead me.'" After several survey trips and an internship, she believed God led her to Haiti, where she serves to this day.

> "Dissatisfaction with life as it was, and a desire to do that which God designed my soul to do, made my heart sing. That was God's calling for me."

A young, millennial couple shared a more pragmatic view. "We looked at the cookie-cutter lifestyle of American living and thought, 'We don't want to waste our lives living for something few ever realize: the American dream.'" Then the young wife added, "And from what I've seen, the American dream costs you your soul." They faithfully serve on their field, going into their eighth year now.

Nuts?

I remember sharing with my unchurched mother God's touch upon me to become a missionary. I was seventeen at the time. She looked straight at me and replied, "Bud, that's just nuts!"

My experience is not unique. It resonates with many serving around the world. When crazy seems the only normal thing to do, perhaps "crazy" constitutes the missionary calling. At seventeen, missionary service didn't seem crazy at all. Today, at sixty-one, it still appears to be my best and only option.

Numerous missionaries share similar thoughts when conversing with friends and family members. A young missionary candidate stated, "Oh, my friends think I'm absolutely out of my mind to go. I think they're out of their minds to stay."

Compassion

Compassion moved another person to "surrender" for missionary service. She shared, "When I saw the need, those children, the suffering, I thought, 'How can I ever go back and just live in my comfortable lifestyle again?'"

Probably one of my favorite exchanges involved an older woman whose husband died. She shared, "I didn't want to sit around the rest of my life looking for something to do. I've got some money my husband left me and Social Security." Where is she today? You'll find her in Honduras loving and caring for little orphan children. She lives as a Honduran on minimal finances, claiming it's the best decision she ever made. What was the catalyst? Her compassion for the orphan children of Honduras.

Missionary, What Moves You?

The missionary calling is as diverse as missionaries themselves. Every experience is different. In some way, each shares a unique touch of God to enter missionary service. Yet each bears a similarity. As Isaiah responded to the Lord's words, "Whom shall I send, and who will go for us? Then said I, Here am I; send me" (Isaiah 6:8 KJV).

However one defines the missionary calling, God somehow moves upon individuals in unique and diverse ways to propel their minds and souls toward missionary service.

What moves you?

Considerations

1. What does moves you?

2. Describe your missionary calling.

3. How is God enabling you for service?

4. What hinders you from moving forward?

(6)

When You Get Hurt

The Rite of Missionary Passage

"Out of suffering have emerged the strongest souls;
the most massive characters are seared with scars."

Kahlil Gibran

The year 2000 marked fifty years of existence for the Baptist Bible Fellowship International. A national meeting was held in Fort Worth, Texas, to celebrate the anniversary.

Our mission's director requested several missionaries bring guests from their perspective fields. My director asked me to bring an old Zulu gentleman who cared for many Zulu congregations throughout the mountains of KwaZulu Natal, South Africa.

His name was Umdlandlankhulu Dube. Most just called him "Simon." Umdlandlankhulu is a bit of a mouthful.

Simon taught me his language, introduced me to his people, and became a close friend. Traveling to America marked a highlight of his life. Toward the end of our trip, after speaking to over one thousand American pastors,

> "American Christians, they doesn't know how to suffer."

visiting several churches, and meeting some of my family members, I asked Simon, "What do you think of America?" His answer sobered our conversation, leading me in an unexpected direction. He responded in his broken English, "American Christians, they doesn't know how to suffer."

When You Get Hurt

I often ask bright, talented, new missionary candidates, "What will you do when you get hurt?" A blank stare usually follows. Then they respond, "What do you mean?"

I reply something like: "When you will get hurt. When you're threatened. Or when you come home to your house on the field to find your safe place is no longer safe due to burglars. Or bandits waylay you in front of your own home, assaulting you so severely that it will take months to physically heal and years to mentally recover. Maybe—like one missionary friend of mine who still serves in Kenya—you'll be shot in the head. Or you'll come out one morning to discover another pickup truck is gone. Two trucks stolen now—just grips me to pieces! Or the missionary friendship you valued so highly suffers an irreparable separation. Then there's malaria—if you're going to Africa. Dengue fever if you're going to the tropics. Oh, and let's not forget about the stress! Stress will put one over on you, let me tell you. Your spouse may die. What if your best missionary friend is gunned down before your very eyes? And what if you're kidnapped? Missionary, what will you do when you get hurt? And what about all the suffering? All the sick children? All the dying? The killing? The bloodshed? The political unrest? The crime? What about all of that? What will you do?"

Someone once warned, "You're going to scare missionary candidates away." But I thought, "That's better than sending them unprepared to the field."

Missionary, you will get hurt. Count on it. It's a rough, hostile place out there. And may I let you in on a little secret? The place to which you're going is controlled by the enemy. An enemy who hates the Father and will do anything—*anything*—to prevent people from coming to him through his Son, Jesus.

Count the cost, or, like so many, you'll leave the field before you even get started. Think about it. Isn't missionary service an incursion into the enemy's—Satan's—stronghold to rescue souls away from him? A veteran missionary shared, "Serving as a missionary in a foreign country is like going to war. The battle is real." You're going to the frontlines of battle. What happens at ground zero? Don't combatants get injured? Don't some die? You'll get hurt. Expect it. Prepare for it. Commit to it.

> Missionary life is an incursion into the enemy's stronghold to rescue souls away from him.

Scripture tells us we are in a war. "For we wrestle not against flesh and blood, but against principalities, against powers, against the rulers of the darkness of this world, against spiritual wickedness in high places" (Ephesians 6:12 KJV).

Do you think you will enter the front lines of battle, and remain uninjured, unhindered, and completely secure? Missionary, you're going to get hurt. Count on it. Plan on it. Ask yourself, "How am I going to deal with my injuries?"

When I pastored in Minnesota, prayer meetings revolved around people's illnesses, needs for better jobs, additional income, and

Grandma Betty's lactose intolerance—I didn't make that last one up. Most prayers centered upon easing people's hurts and discomforts.

Every Thursday morning, a group of retired men met for prayer breakfast. They were a wonderful group of old guys. I loved talking with them, laughing, and sharing life. Their prayer time, however, irked me into senselessness.

Every Thursday, their many prayer requests centered upon their physical afflictions. Eating grits while an old guy is talking about his bleeding goiter is, well . . . .

And then there's the other old guy that always needed to rehearse his many trips to the ER. Open sores, prostates, bunions, hernias, and more—it went on and on and on. It put a whole new twist on that piece of cinnamon toast dripping with hot butter I was trying to eat. It just sort of sat there on the plate, transforming into anything else but a delectable piece of morning toast.

Maladies of the most personal nature were shared. Once an old fellow asked for prayer. He shared, "My hemorrhoids are really tearing me up this week; pray for me." This was after a morning breakfast of scrambled eggs, hash browns, Tabasco, and applesauce.

I blurted out, "Let's lay hands on those rhoids and pray for healing." Not a single guy laughed. This was typical of those wonderful cold-land Scandinavian descended people. I, however, chuckled for the rest of the day.

We continued with psoriasis, arthritis, diabetes, slipped discs, headaches, colonoscopies, and other such issues. It felt a bit like a leper colony at times.

Never once mentioned was, "God, please show me how my suffering can make me more like you." Or, "God, in my suffering show me someone I can help through my anguish." Or, "God, help me become more like your Son in his sufferings. Help us reach this community for you, oh, God." Never once.

You're Going to the Front Lines

Strongholds of darkness exist out there. You're going to the front lines far beyond lactose intolerance. The enemy has a plan for you. His aim is to shoot you out of the saddle. He desires to seriously wound you rendering you unfit for service.

Much of American evangelical Christianity functions from the idea that, "The safest place to be is in the center of God's will." I've heard it a thousand times ad nauseam.

Hey, guess what? The most *dangerous* place to be is in the center of God's will. The enemy tolerates little of submissive, God-pleasing servants, of God-seeking, God-serving followers of the Way.

The idea of being in the "center of God's will" meaning that no ills will befall you is not close to reality. Have you ever read the Bible? Jesus didn't say, "Take up your comfort and follow me."

Hudson Taylor, the great nineteenth-century missionary to China, battled depression his entire ministry.[11] Adoniram Judson, pioneer missionary to Burma, said, "If I had not felt certain that every additional trial was ordered by infinite love and mercy, I could not have survived my accumulated sufferings."[12]

I still remember the news breaking of the missionaries and their children massacred in Zimbabwe in 1987.[13] We had been in South Africa only one year when that news came on the TV. My son looked at said, "Daddy, will that happen to us?"

Here's an important point of consideration. There's a lot of suffering, traumatized people out in the missionary ranks. I know, because I'm one of them. In my book *To Hell, Back, and Beyond – A PTSD Journey: When Faith and Trauma Collide*, I share my personal crash-and-burn trauma. The good news is that Kathy and I are back up on our feet serving as missionaries again in a wonderful capacity, for which God prepared us through all our sufferings. Suffering and missionary service go hand in hand.

The evangelical theology of suffering focuses too much—in my opinion—on the comfort of the individual. A common response to discomfort by many American Christians is: "Why? Why me? I'm serving you, God. I'm loving you, God. How come this has happened to me?"

> Suffering and missionary service go hand in hand.

My answer is, "What makes you so different from Job, Joseph, Moses, David, Isaiah, Esther, and a host of other people mentioned at the end of Hebrews 11?

Consider the apostle Peter. He asked to be crucified upside down—or so legend has it—because he thought himself unworthy of suffering like Jesus had.

"But, God, why me? I've prayed in your name. I love you. I give my offerings. I have faith. I'm making this huge missionary sacrifice in your name. I'm doing this great work in your name. Why did you let this happen to me?"

In contrast, during my twenty-two years in South Africa, never once did I hear a Zulu Christian ask such a question. Suffering was part of life. Deal with it. Find God in it. Move forward.

As I write these very words, tough news came about a friend. After a long career as a firefighter, he retired a year ago. This morning he dropped dead of a heart attack in his driveway. We spent a great weekend together at a men's retreat just a few months ago. He was a faithful member of his church. Yet he's gone.

You'll Get Hurt—Count on It—Prepare for It

For American missionaries, sometimes the health and wealth gospel derails us by playing a diabolical part in our preconceived notions about serving God on the mission field. The thought is, "If I serve God, he will protect me no matter what." The problem with such a viewpoint is that it is contrary to the Scriptures and disproven by at least one hundred people in the Bible. Suffering is part of God's plan for his people (2 Corinthians 1:4).

Gregory Peck's sobering words in the 1961 blockbuster movie *The Guns of Navarone* resembles a more sobering truth of missionary service. Faced in WWII with attacking two superguns in the mountains on a fictitious island held by the Germans, Peck—playing Captain Keith Mallory—tries to sober up the men he leads by stating, "You're in it now, up to your neck."

Missionary, you'll be betrayed. Expect it. Loneliness is many a missionary's constant companion. Those hero missionaries you admired during your visits to the field now will appear frail and human.

The citizens of your chosen field will resist forming friendships. Governmental red tape alone may push you to the edge sometimes. Absence from your family's events back home becomes a painful cross you must carry.

When you return to your country of birth, you'll find that your family and friends have moved on. Oh, they still care and love you, but a disconnect develops during your absence. You're always the guest. The visitor. As a missionary, you'll grow into a different person. Home feels less like home, and on the field you're always the foreigner.

You'll most likely suffer sickness. Multiple times. Illness may become a constant companion.

Missionaries share stories of physical assaults, robberies, home invasions, and hijackings. A missionary last week shared with me, "We've been robbed twice and burglarized five times during our missionary career."

Some will suffer inhumane traumas. Others—like me—will suffer mental overloads from the suffering, carnage, and killing going on all around them. Missionary life will change you forever. Yet I would do it all over again.

Count Your Cost

It's important to understand that missionary service exacts a high price. It is wise to count the cost of such a life.

A large crowd was following Jesus. He turned around and said to them, "'If you want to be my disciple, you must, by comparison, hate everyone else—your father and mother, wife and children, brothers and sisters—yes, even your own life. Otherwise, you cannot be my disciple. And if you do not carry your own cross and follow me, you cannot be my disciple. But don't begin until you count the cost. For who would begin construction of a building without first calculating the cost to see if there is enough money to finish it? Otherwise, you might complete only the foundation before running out of money, and then everyone would laugh at you. They would say, 'There's the person who started that building and couldn't afford to finish it!'" (Luke 14:25-30)

Accept it, expect it, and prepare yourself for it. This is your cross, missionary. Suffering is real. If anything, we suffer more than friends and family back home because of our exposures to multiple unsafe environments. Are you willing to carry such a cross?

Suffering—Even for Ministry—Is Not Easy

Although missionaries experience wonderful, happy, and fulfilling events on the field, a single event can quickly change our perspectives. When trauma arises, it sometimes acts like a black hole sucking all the good stuff out of your attitude. All that seems to remain is the trauma: That thing that happened to you.

What will you do when you get hurt? How will you respond? What about the follow-up afterward?

I believe thinking through this issue now will greatly help you when you eventually experience something traumatic.

During my years as a fire/police chaplain in Minnesota, we offered critical incident stress management for police and firefighters who experienced tragic events. This often involved the gruesome death of a child during a callout on the scene.

Helping firefighters work through grief and stress both before and after painful events gave them the means to survive their initial trauma. They worked through it and lived with it, functioning as effective firefighters and human beings.

It was while helping firefighters deal with their trauma that I started to realize I'd not dealt with mine. Missionaries often suffer debilitation after a harsh event affects them.

A passage of Scripture that helped me much is found towards the end of Hebrews 11. Missionary, look and consider deeply the immense suffering God's witnesses experienced in times long ago.

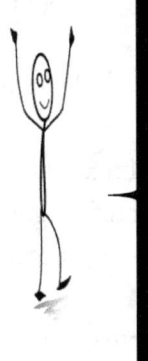

> How much more do I need to say? It would take too long to recount the stories of the faith of Gideon, Barak, Samson, Jephthah, David, Samuel, and all the prophets. By faith these people overthrew kingdoms, ruled with justice, and received what God had promised them. They shut the mouths of lions, quenched the flames of fire, and escaped death by the edge of the sword. Their weakness was turned to strength. They became strong in battle and put whole armies to flight. Women received their loved ones back again from death. (Hebrews 11:32-35)

That's not the end of the story.

> **But others** were tortured, refusing to turn from God in order to be set free. They placed their hope in a better life after the resurrection. Some were jeered at, and their backs were cut open with whips. Others were chained in prisons. Some died by stoning, some were sawed in half, and others were killed with the sword. Some went about wearing skins of sheep and goats, destitute and oppressed and mistreated. They were too good for this world, wandering over deserts and mountains, hiding in caves and holes in the ground. (Hebrews 11:35-38, emphasis added)

When Your Feelings Get Hurt

Hurt feelings. Apart from the obvious persecution that comes from those who opposed the gospel, missionaries often talk about another kind of hurt.

Does it surprise you to learn that much hurt—most hurt—described by many missionaries revolves around their hurt feelings? Beelzebub knows right where to hit us. You know, that experience occurring when another person, church, or organization – doesn't affirm us in the way we desire.

They really offended me. Many conversations with missionaries revolve around their offendedness by other individuals. These individuals are often other missionaries, donors, pastors, or team members failing to support us in the ways expected.

"They hurt my feelings."
"They don't appreciate me."
"They don't value me."
"The team I'm on is toxic."
"I don't like them."
"They ignored me."
"The younger missionaries don't respect me."
"I feel like I'm nothing here."

The list can go on, and on, and on. When missionaries define their hurt in this manner, then wild, overreactive contemplations follow.

That's it. I'm finished. "We are going to resign, go back to the States, and work secular jobs." Really? After raising your funds, finishing your schooling and training, and arriving on your field, you're just going to quit? Because someone hurt your feelings? Really? How many years of preparation have you undergone? And you're just going to hang it up after only how many months? And what about the next challenge you encounter in life? What will you do then?

"Well, we are going to resign and find another missions agency." Really? You will brand and stereotype an entire organization over your hurt feelings? What happens if you find another agency, and your feeling get hurt again? (Spoiler: They will.)

"We've decided to quit missions and quit everything" (this usually includes church) "because my feelings were so hurt. I was undervalued. Used up. Discarded. I'm done."

So you are going to quit God, leave Christ, abandon the body because frail, fallen human beings in the church act like frail, fallen human beings in the church?

By the way, how are you acting right now?

When meeting with other missionary care leaders from other organizations, I've learned that these unfortunate exchanges take place all too often. It brings me to ask this probing question.

When your hurt becomes your idol. When your first consideration above all else becomes your hurt, and only your hurt, doesn't your hurt then become an idol? Expecting everyone else to be uber-sensitive about your feelings lest you get hurt—that's an idol. Right? Or am I way off here? When you expect others to bow in deference to your sensitivities, that's idolatry—right?

As the sun in the universe of your feelings, all the other people-planets in your soul-system must revolve around you. When people fail to orbit your elliptical sensitivities, your soul spins out of alignment. Overreactive decisions often follow. Then an emotional black hole appears, sucking all reality out of your personal soul-system.

See your hurts as growth opportunities. I know that sounds a bit sappy and over-spiritualized. Yet as I read the Bible, it seems to me that in hurts lie opportunities for forgiveness, patience, and spiritual growth.

A worst-case scenario is that your hurt will weaken you. But maybe weakness is the realm where God wants you to exist. Depending upon God and allowing Christ to work in us—even in our hurts—can grow into a God-experience, depending upon our response.

What's your response to that person who hurt you? As a God-called missionary, here's an injunction for us to follow:

> Is there any encouragement from belonging to Christ? Any comfort from his love? Any fellowship together in the Spirit? Are your hearts tender and compassionate? Then make me truly happy by agreeing wholeheartedly with each other, loving one another, and working together with one mind and purpose. Don't be selfish; don't try to impress others. Be humble, thinking of others as better than yourselves. Don't look out only for your own interests, but take an interest in others, too. (Philippians 2:1-4)

Safe, Healing Harbors

Upon returning in 2006 to Minnesota to pastor, I didn't understand the level of my malady. In my fifth year of pastoring, I called my pastor friend Randy. Randy pastored Constance Free Church in Andover, Minnesota, for over thirty years.

After a long talk in his office, he said, "Don, I don't think this is about pastoring. I don't know what's going on, but I think you've brought something back with you from your experiences as a missionary in Africa. Maybe even before Africa."

With strong, loving encouragement, I began seeing a Christian therapist—which was a huge initial dent to my ego—and began a process of unraveling a maze of traumatic carnage in my life. I was diagnosed with Post-Traumatic Stress Disorder (PTSD).

Generous people donated to a fund to aid pastors needing help. I never paid a penny for all my sessions and learning how to manage my PTSD opened a new—although painful—opportunity to serve.

Finding Safe Harbors

When I began trying to share my nightmares, hypersensitivity to noise, and other issues, people didn't know how to react. How could they? Several pastors I reached out to disengaged very quickly.

While the local church retains a responsibility for the welfare of its missionaries, many churches sadly use sending organizations in a manner that looks more like abdication than delegation of missionary care.[14] Although there are some excellent churches out there who care deeply for their missionaries, they regrettably are few and far between.

The church is an easy target at which to hurl our disappointments. "The church did this or that to me," marks a common accusation. Here's what I came to understand. My home church couldn't respond to my needs because they didn't possess the experience or skills to do so. After all, how much can an American pastor or congregation understand about a missionary's life?

I once shared with some people in Wisconsin our concern for the rampant crime and unrest sweeping South Africa. By that time, we'd lost a dozen church members to murder. A host of other experiences occurred, including brutal assaults of our members, loss of homes, and rape. The body count of people dying due to AIDS climbed. And then there were the children: those beautiful children. Monthly, we'd conduct funerals for children who died of some illness. Often, when showing up to a

> Looking for solace among people who know little about missionary suffering is often a dead-end.

crowded cemetery, we'd conduct our graveside service with a dozen other groups also burying their dead in close rows of trenches.

When trying to share such an experience, a member of that church in Wisconsin piped up saying, "Oh, we know about crime! Someone else was murdered down in Milwaukee this week."

Looking for solace among people who know little about missionary suffering is often a dead-end.

Understand, Pastors Hurt, Too

If you're expecting your home church pastor to tend to your wounds when you're ailing in missionary life, then understand this. Pastors are some of the most abused, mistreated people on the planet. They carry enormous weight caring for their congregations. Your pastor may be too extended, without much mental or spiritual margin to help.

Pastoring ten years in two medium-sized churches of 300 to 400 people taught me much about an American pastor's life. After a week of committee meetings, counseling sessions, two funerals, sermon preparation, staff luncheon, complaining members, budgets, ministry teams, and the rest, little time or energy existed to entertain anything else. People stretched me so thin that I felt like a sheet of wax paper.

Missionaries reach out to their pastors seeking for help that most pastors are not trained, experienced, or qualified to give. Many pastors don't have a brim of time or emotion to wade into a missionary's deep waters.

As someone who served over twenty years in South Africa and spent nearly ten years pastoring in Minnesota, I can tell you that many pastors don't know what to say or do in this area. It's outside their context of life and ministry. And many pastors live as broken vessels themselves.

Understanding this is essential to avoid a critical or hurtful spirit. To be honest, many American churches today are too busy and out of touch with real missions work to care about missionaries anyway. Yes, they take their short-term mission trips, but they often focus on their experience of their trip and not on the workers in the fields of that place.

Ask God to help you find safe harbors to heal. Remember, if we ask anything in his will and name, he will bring it to us.

Talk with Other Missionaries

The missionary experience is unique. It's often not possible for a non-missionary to understand a missionary any more than it's possible for a non-PTSD sufferer to understand those suffering from PTSD. Katie Gillian comments well here:

> Acceptance of the injury and the fact that it is part of who you are now is the biggest challenge to be honest. I have never had to do this as I have never known a time when I wasn't a bit cracked, a lot cracked . . . For those who knew what it was to have an unbroken brain, I feel immensely empathetic towards the struggle to accept this.[15]

Our family, friends, and supporters live in different contexts than we do. How can they understand a life from which they are unfamiliar and so far removed? Friends often do the best they can, but we can't expect any more—although we often need much more. This can cause missionaries great frustration.

Finding a caring missionary with a good listening ear who holds a high level of confidentiality is perhaps one the best things you can do. Another is to seek and find help from those who are trained to help.

Think through Your Theology of Suffering

Jesus healed only a few during his earthly days. Many others also suffered sickness, assaults, depression, and deprivation during his ministry; yet not all were healed.

A view of suffering that says, "God, you must take this away from me because . . ." may be spiritually shortsighted.

During my diagnosis and treatment for PTSD, my view of suffering changed considerably. I went from asking God, "Why?" to a different set of questions.

Where is God in this? Our struggle is often to see God as an active participant in our suffering. It's amazing how quickly we—especially we missionaries—develop an agnostic view of God in our personal suffering. "God, where are you? Do you really care? Why don't you answer my prayers? Are you there? Really?"

God is there. Nothing happens by accident. God doesn't fall asleep, then awake and say, "Oh, sorry, Don, I missed that one!" Perhaps the reason for seemingly unanswered prayers are that God's plans for your suffering far outweigh simple alleviation of your pain.

Before my treatment for PTSD, I'd turned into a functioning Christian agnostic. You know, the attitude of, "I know God is there. He just isn't very concerned about me right now."

But I developed a truer and healthier view. Rather than begging, "Please, please, please, God, take it away," my personal prayer centered on, "Father, help me see your plan in this. How you are working. What you are striving to accomplish in and through my suffering. The suffering of others, for that matter."

How can I draw closer to Christ in personal suffering? If my suffering can help me draw closer to Jesus, then suffering takes on new purpose. When viewing suffering through the eyes of Jesus as he hung on that cross during those horrible hours of agony, my suffering melds into identification with Christ instead of just focusing on me. Isaiah's words in Isaiah 53:3-4 chapter bear rich reflection.

> He was despised and rejected—
>   a man of sorrows, acquainted with deepest grief.
> We turned our backs on him and looked the other way.
>   He was despised, and we did not care.
> Yet it was our weaknesses he carried;
>   it was our sorrows that weighed him down.

How does my suffering equip me for a higher task? Today my sweet wife Kathy and I serve as missionaries. As a PTSD survivor, I endeavor to help missionaries survive, thrive, and serve longer and stronger in their fields of calling. This is possible partly because of our missionary experience and suffering. In this, suffering proves purposeful. Beyond just pain, loss, and discomfort, suffering gives reason to serve. Recently, a friend asked Kathy, "How can Don help missionaries when he has this PTSD thing?" Kathy responded, "It's because of his PTSD that we can help other missionaries, not in spite of it."

> Suffering has purpose beyond just pain, loss, and discomfort.

How does my weakness help me become stronger? The apostle Paul stated it this way when writing about his own sufferings:

> I want to know Christ and experience the mighty power that raised him from the dead. I want to suffer with him, sharing in his death, so that one way or another I will experience the resurrection from the dead! (Philippians 3:10-11)

See your suffering as a gift. What did you just say? Deep into our weekly sessions, my Christian therapist Tom posed a question:

"Don, can you see the gift God has given you here?" My facial reaction caused him to offer a follow-up question. "Don," he continued, "what do you think about that question?" I responded, "You don't really want to know." Tom pressed. I continued, "I think you're a blinking idiot for asking that question." Tom smiled.

A year later, Kathy and I sat with Darlene, a family therapist, discussing my PTSD, its effects on our relationship, and how we could manage it together. She asked that same question: "Do you see the gift God has given you?"

All those night sweats. Sleep deprivation. Hypersensitivity to noise—still a problem for me. Sleep terrors. Physical pain. Avoidance. Mood swings. My hyper, startled reactions—still a problem. And the list can go on. Yeah, what a gift!

But good things developed in all of this! I found empathy for suffering people, greater capacity for compassion with people, and humility. We created our ministry, Missionary to Missionary Care. Thank you, God. My sitting here today, typing these words, might never have occurred apart from the suffering I experienced.

Suffering serves a God-purpose in your life. There are three passages on which I lean heavily these days:

> Each time he said, "My grace is all you need. My power works best in weakness." So now I am glad to boast about my weaknesses, so that the power of Christ can work through me. That's why I take pleasure in my weaknesses, and in the insults, hardships, persecutions, and troubles that I suffer for Christ. For when I am weak, then I am strong. (2 Corinthians 12:9-10)

These words of Paul uniquely apply to me. Look again at the passage above. Note the truths leaping off the page.

1. "Each time . . ." – Go to God often with your hurt.
2. "My grace . . ." – God's answer and care are always sourced in his loveliness and purpose for our lives.
3. "My power works best . . ." – It's all about God's supremacy to accomplish his task, in his ways, according to his reasons.
4. ". . . works best in weakness." – This is the opposite of human nature, teaching, and preaching. Missionary, here's a harsh but possible truth:

Much of God's purpose in your ministry may be to find accomplishment in your weakest, sickest, most hurtful moments. During these times, one learns to rely deeply upon God.

5. "So now I am glad to boast about my weaknesses."

Hang on, Paul! Just wait a minute! You're glad to boast about *what*? This sort of reminds me of George Bailey in the classic movie *It's a Wonderful Life*, when George says to the corrupt grumpy old bugger Mr. Potter, "Just a minute—just a minute. Now, hold on, Mr. Potter. Just a minute."

I sort of feel that way with Paul here.

Now, hold on just a minute, Paul! You're glad to boast about your weaknesses? What is wrong with you? Anyways you're supposed to say that, because you're the great apostle Paul.

6. ". . . so that the power of Christ can work through me."

Here's Paul's reasoning. In weakness, God receives the splendor of our labors. More than our prayer letters, updates, presentations, PowerPoints, clever fundraising, and glowing reports, *God gets the glory* when we're flat on our backs in weakness. And, missionary, glory—God getting his due—is what it's all about.

7. "That's why I take pleasure in my weaknesses, and in the insults, hardships, persecutions, and troubles that I suffer for Christ."

Learn to take pleasure in your weaknesses. When you suffer weakness, insults will come from a select few. But they are usually only a few. Cold shoulders. Callous comments. Accusations. Insinuations. Hardships. Trouble. It's all there in our modern context.

Few donors desire to hear of the missionaries' weaknesses. Contributors want stories of progress. Paul's standard here might prove difficult to raise financial support in our modern-day context. Weakness is not what supporters want to hear. It's not what they want to support.

This is perhaps one reason we fear sharing a shred of genuine feebleness and struggle with supporters and churches.

Often, when I share my fight with PTSD, the reception is cold. A person asking, "So, what caused your PTSD?" doesn't understand—thankfully—the nature of PTSD. Such pain is rarely casually talked about. I found that in *To Hell, Back, and Beyond – A PTSD Journey: When Faith and Trauma Collide,* it was possible to write about the experiences I still to this day can barely talk about.

Thankfully, a few rugged champions—scarred themselves—now support and encourage me. But if you decide to be a Paul about your weaknesses, get ready for rejection.

While meeting with a pastor over lunch to discuss our new missionary ministry, Missionary to Missionary Care, he shot back: "Why did you quit and come off the field the first time?"

I thought, "You dummy. Leaving after twenty-two years spent in the field is not quitting. We give our soldiers a pension for the rest of their lives for serving that amount of time. What in the . . . are you talking about?"

Sitting in his massive air-conditioned office, I replied, "Quit? What do you mean 'quit'?"

"Yes," he said. "Quit. When you resigned from South Africa in 2006. Why did you decide to come off the field?"

"Well, I was finished," I said. "Worn out. Sick. And I needed a break. I found out that I needed some professional help, too."

He replied, "I never quit anything in my life."

That ended the conversation.

One "biblical counselor"—also a missionary—offered me his wealth of wisdom from his thimbleful of knowledge. "Don, your problem is you think too much of yourself. There's no such thing as PTSD. You're centering yourself too much upon yourself. Get off yourself and just focus upon God, and your problems will go away."

Seeing his back as he carried himself away pompously, I turned to Kathy and said, "Don't worry about it. That's all he knows."

When it comes to speaking about mental health many evangelicals become medieval in their attitude and responses.

Fortunately, God brought some incredible church leaders alongside of us in our journey. Their encouragement and support are much appreciated.

Suffering creates empathy with other sufferers. A missionary once shared publicly about a brutal assault he suffered at the hands of thugs in the country he served. He asked me in front of a group of thirty people, "How am I ever going to get over this?"

I replied: "You never will. That's who you are now. That's what God will use to accomplish his purpose in and through you. Now you must discover the person God is creating in you through your suffering."

A woman named Kate, whom I follow online, suffers from complex PTSD. She writes in her blog, *Kate Gillie Art*:

> I believe, those of us who live with PTSD are simply better humans. We have suffered and suffer, it makes us humble and open to the pain of others, we find our salvation in supporting others.[16]

Early in my life and ministry, every spiritual gifts assessment I took rated me at a zero for the gift of mercy, empathy, and understanding of others' suffering. Not anymore.

Recently, a similar assessment I took rated me at 9 out of 10 for mercy and empathy. So you see, suffering can powerfully and positively transform us.

Prepare for hurt. It's coming your way. Just last week, we sat with a missionary couple. Few ministries match the unique effectiveness of this duo. The missionary wife shared, "When they recruit you to become missionaries, they make you believe it's like their amazing, glowing reports—you know, like the short-term mission trips they take—like what they share with churches. But it's not like that at all. It's *way* different! They don't tell you about the struggles, loneliness, living out of a suitcase, raising your kids between two cultures—that kind of stuff."

My encouragement to you comes from my own rugged journey. Seek God as you walk through your valley of the shadow of death. Remember, it's a shadow, not a reality. A shadow—the projection of a thing, not the thing itself—is always bigger than the obstacle itself. Seek God in the shadows of your life. Trust him in those shadows. You may find that the challenge facing you is not that great of a challenge after all. Learn to find God in your shadows, because that's where God promises, "I am with you."

Considerations

1. What suffering are you experiencing now?

2. On a suffering-scale of one to ten (ten being the harshest), where are you now?

3. Where can you see God's love in your suffering?

4. How is God leading and directing you through your suffering?

5. What will you do when you get hurt?

(7)

Loneliness

"I pray that no missionary will ever be
as lonely as I have been."

Lottie Moon,
Baptist missionary to China from 1873 to 1912

"Pain, as C.S. Lewis said, is God's megaphone ('He whispers to us in our joys, speaks to us in our conscience, and shouts to us in our pain').
The pain of loneliness is
one way in which He wants to get our attention."

by Elisabeth Elliot, *The Path of Loneliness*

Loneliness—as a missionary—is a cross you'll need to learn to carry. Sorry, there's no other way around it. The missionary life requires experiencing seasons of loneliness. Yet your loneliness can present positive opportunities.

I like Ivane Luna's writing on the subject:

"Loneliness is magnified on the mission field, especially when involved in cross-cultural missions. We are in a foreign country, away from family, away from little luxuries and comforts that we are used to. Most likely, we are surrounded by people speaking a language that is not our own. We don't have the same strong support structure that we would have back home. Loneliness is not a phenomenon exclusive to people on the mission field, but I believe that it's one of the reasons why we can find such disheartening statistics regarding missionary attrition. . . .Loneliness feeds into disheartening statistics regarding missionary attrition."[17]

Loneliness Is Not a Sin

Loneliness is a natural response to a vacuum of human need. Once you arrive on your field, a void is created by the absence of friends, family, and support structures. This is normal. Learn to expect it. Plan to embrace it.

How you adjust to your loneliness will greatly affect your soul's health and the welfare of those around you. This is the number two problem cited by most younger missionaries contacting us for help. Assuring them that they've not committed the unpardonable sin by being lonely is, in itself, helpful.

Time of Adjustment

The simple act of transitioning from your country of birth to a new place is an adjustment. Loneliness is part of that process. View your loneliness as adjusting to your God-adventure. Great adventurers are great because they willingly venture out into hazards few ever contemplate. Few—if any—explorers ever traveled with all their family and friends. Loneliness is the inevitable result of living such an incredible life.

Jesus Suffered from Loneliness, Too

Loneliness creates opportunities for growth. Isaiah 53:3 uses these words to describe Jesus's suffering:

> He was despised and rejected—
>   a man of sorrows, acquainted with deepest grief.
> We turned our backs on him and looked the other way.
>   He was despised, and we did not care.

Jesus suffered from loneliness, too. A lot of loneliness, in fact. He was rejected by his friends while hanging on that old cross; Jesus understands our loneliness.

When we struggle with loneliness, it's good. It gives us the opportunity to feel the way Jesus felt. To hurt the way Jesus hurt. To cry the way Jesus cried: "My God, my God, why have you abandoned me?" (Matthew 27:46).

Whether perceived or actual, loneliness is a separation from those who are closest to us. It's sometimes the perception that all who claim to love and care about us have abandoned us.

Partings and goodbyes become part of a missionary's emotional DNA. It never gets easier. For me, the "goodbyes" grow more difficult.

Often, the last event a missionary experiences is a gathering of family, friends, or church members. Celebrations, words, and hugs are exchanged. Days later, the new missionary steps off the plane in a new country where he or she is surrounded only by strangers.

Yet in all the "goodbyes" are opportunities to painfully grow and identify with our Savior, who suffered separation, too.

Your Loneliness as an Incense to God

Remember the Old Testament burnt offerings? The Bible often records that the burnt offerings of those days formed a sweet-smelling savor to God.

I think missionary loneliness is a bit like that. Offering your loneliness to God in honor of him and in service to others as a contribution of gratitude gives your loneliness purpose. When you are lonely, try to reflect upon God. Don't waste your loneliness in aloneness.

Connect Deeply with Jesus

Loneliness creates margin in our lives to draw us closer to God. The busy lifestyles we leave back home fill souls with so many things other than God.

Use your solitude to draw closer to the one who gives you eternal life. The Bible speaks often about finding solitude to meet with God. Missionary service can provide a wonderful opportunities for God and you to spend quality time together.

If you're an American missionary, you might find solitude a daunting task. Busyness can drive us recklessly through life. Many young missionaries share their boredom during their first years on the field. "I was used to being busy all the time," one missionary commented.

Boredom is a call to solitude and aloneness with God. It's a huge, lacking discipline in many Christian's lives, as we live in this noisy, breakneck-pace society we call America.

Don't fear loneliness. Embrace it. Make it submit to a positive purpose in your life and soul. Loneliness can become your friend.

Considerations

1. Describe your loneliness.

2. Where is God in your loneliness?

3. How can your loneliness draw you closer to the people you serve?

4. How can your loneliness become holiness?

(8)

Missionary Failure
The Lack of Soul-Care

Many mission sending agencies offer a host of reasons—perceived or factual—for the many missionary failures in their agency. But I think "failure" is far too broad a word.

Often, for an individual who is serving—whether for a few years or for decades—, transitions will occur in their life. Simply leaving the field is not failure. To me, missionaries defines their failures themselves. Many missionaries returning home talk in terms of their disappointments. They stumble apologetically upon the reasons for their departure from the field. But much of our missionary failure is due to a lack of good soul-care.

> Much of our missionary failure is due to lack of good soul-care.

Soul-care can seemingly exist in a vacuum of theological mumbo jumbo. We talk about eschatology, ecclesiology, soteriology, angelology, bibliology, premillennialism, postmillennialism, amillennialism, rapture, universal, Reformed, Charismatic, Baptist, Catholic, Methodist, Lutheran, Presbyterian, interdenominational, nondenominational, cross-denominational, Calvinist, Arminian, apocalyptic, grace-based, hyper-grace, dispensational, covenant, orthodox, organized, reorganized, and . . . the beat goes on. Yet when was the last time you heard anything about what Jesus describe as, "Is anything worth more than your soul?" (Mark 8:37).

What about Your Soul-Health?

How does one ensure soul-health even in the most adverse winds and waves of life and ministry? How goes your soul at this very moment?

A brief examination of Jesus's famous words in Mark 8 and Matthew 16 shows the ultimate importance of our souls. Jesus said, "And what do you benefit if you gain the whole world but lose your own soul? Is anything worth more than your soul?" (Matthew 16:26; Mark 8:36-37).

> Is anything worth more than your soul? Anything?

This verse must rank as one of the most important verses in all the Bible. Yet the topic is rarely discussed. Soul-care—though little talked about—is a high priority for Jesus.

It was during one of Jesus's busy ministry campaigns that he began to reveal the purpose for his coming: "Then Jesus began to tell them that the Son of Man must suffer many terrible things and be rejected . . ." (Mark 8:31).

The Greek language in which Jesus spoke these words seems to indicate that Jesus held nothing back. He plainly revealed all. These words are in the imperfect Greek tense, which shows that Jesus probably repeated them more than once.[18]

Peter interrupted—as was his impulsive nature—and censured Jesus severely: "How dare you, Jesus! Who do you think you are? This will never happen! It's not in my plans, Jesus!"

I wonder how often we, as missionaries, pastors, and church leaders, do the same. Stand back Jesus and watch us do our god-stuff!

Christ connected with a right hook on Peter's misguided soul. The knockout blow hit squarely. "Get behind me, Satan!" he said to Peter (Mark 8:33 NIV).

In other words, he was saying: There's more going on here than just you, Peter! This is my father's plan for my life—and yours, by the way. It is his plan for the whole world.

Peter, not yet a career missionary—he was still fulfilling his internship—,was self-intentioned, self-aligned, and self-guided. He crumbled.

Jesus's words rang out: Peter, stop trying to hang onto your own life! Lose your ambitions for the sake my ambitions!

Peter simply did not understand the plan. How could he? Peter's go-get-em tactics to win the world to Jesus involved Peter himself first and foremost. His plans weren't necessarily bad; they just excluded upcoming God-events and a future he couldn't possibly anticipate. Yet they omitted the very person he claimed to represent.

Jesus then called the crowd to gather with his disciples.

His words probably shocked and puzzled a good many people that day: "If any of you wants to be my follower, you must turn from your selfish ways, take up your cross, and follow me" (Mark 8:34).

Peter revolted at the mention of Christ's death. What? A cross? No way do I want that Roman contraption of suffering and death close to me. No way! I'm into ministry building here! That's not in my plans at all, Jesus. I am getting ready within a year or so to launch the first megachurch of Jesus Christ in Jerusalem. It's going to be big!

Here a question presents itself: Is it possible for people who are deeply committed to God to lose their souls doing God-stuff? Missionary, is it possible that while doing missionary stuff you could lose your own soul in the process, allowing it to dry up so it becomes an inhospitable place?

Jesus's teaching to his disciples seems to indicate this possibility. In all our names, signs, titles, and buildings, maybe Jesus isn't as central to our message and methodology as we assume.

Jesus continues: "If you try to hang on to your life, you will lose it" (Mark 8:35).

Hanging on appears to be the trait of today. Hanging on to my money. Hanging on to my position. Hanging on to my expectations. Hanging on to my structures. Hanging on to my desires. Hanging on to my ministry. Hanging on to my missionary empire, my financial support, my building programs, my fundraising. Hanging on to the way we always did church for the last thirty years.

I suspect many of us plague ourselves by hanging on to good desires to the detriment of our souls. Hanging on to our lives hinders true cross-bearing.

Jesus continued, "you must give up your own way, take up your cross, and follow me." Some that day might have continued to nod their heads in agreement. "Okay, yes, I can do that. I will do that. I think I can do that. Wait, but how do you do that exactly? What do you mean, Jesus? Does that mean I need to forget myself, lose sight of my own interests, and center myself upon something other than just myself? What about my needs, self-care, and self-forgiveness?"

> Many of us plague ourselves by hanging on to good desires to the detriment of our souls.

Jesus said, "Whoever wants to be my disciple must *deny* themselves and take up their cross daily and follow me" (Luke 9:23 NIV).

Jesus used the same word for "denial" when he denounced Peter, declaring, " "I tell you the truth, Peter--this very night, before the rooster crows, you will deny three times that you even know me."

Peter's denial of Jesus was absolute.

As Peter cried out before a group of people gathered around a fire on a cold night, his denouncement of Jesus was resolute. "I do not even know the man!" If we learn to deny ourselves like Peter denied Christ that cold night, we might be on the right track.

Lose my what? That was not the end of Jesus's words that day. His perplexing message continued: "If you try to hang on to your life, you will lose it. But if you give up your life for my sake and for the sake of the Good News, you will save it" (Mark 8:35).

I need to lose my life? What does that mean? How does that work? Why would I want to do that, Jesus?

Jesus demanded his twelve apostles put away their personal aspirations and pick up their crosses instead. Picking up our crosses is the first step in good soul-care. The opposite of cross-bearing is self-bearing.

Here, in my opinion, is one of the most under-grasped passages in all the Bible. Jesus asks a diagnostic question: "And what do you benefit if you gain the whole world but lose your own soul?" (Mark 8:36). Let these words sink into the context of Jesus's other words a bit. What was Jesus saying?

In many Bible teaching churches, this verse is usually applied to salvation: a point and moment of decision. If you don't accept Jesus, invite him into your heart, repent of your sins, and trust him, you will lose your own soul.

But Jesus didn't exactly say that here. Did he?

These words also find application by those who possess less than others. "Don't acquire too much worldly stuff, because by grasping for material things and money you might lose your soul."

Well, but Jesus didn't say that either. Did he?

Jesus continued to clarify: "Is anything worth more than your soul?" (Mark 8:37). Jesus posed a rhetorical question: What is worth more than your soul? I think Jesus was talking more about soul-awareness.

In my younger days I always interpreted this verse as I was instructed:— as a personal decision that impacted where one spent eternity if one compromised the spiritual over earthly things.[19] But that is not exactly within the bounds of good interpretation here. Jesus was not only dealing with an eternal perspective of one's soul. He also called attention to one's current perspective of the soul.[20]

Missionary, what's the condition of your soul at this very moment? Jesus wasn't just making a case for the afterlife in this passage. He presented a clear need for immediate examination of the condition of our souls.[21]

Here's a thought: Is it possible for zealous, busy missionaries to lose themselves in the process of doing their missionary work? To serve for years, only to experience a withering of the soul? Missionaries share that this is too often the case. I know it's true. Personally, I unintentionally allowed my own soul to wither over years of missionary service. I learned the health of your soul is of the highest consideration.

> The health of your soul is your highest consideration.

Considerations

1. How's your soul-health at this very moment?

2. What are your most important goals of life and ministry?

3. Describe your concept of missionary success and failure.

4. What good stuff do you hang on to that may prove detrimental to your soul?

(9)

Soul-Care or Soul-Bare

"One ship drives east and another drives west
With the self-same winds that blow;
'Tis the set of the sails
And not the gales
That tells them the way to go.

Like the winds of the sea are the ways of fate
As we voyage along through life;
'Tis the set of the soul
That decides its goal
And not the calm or the strife."

Ella Wheeler Wilcox, —"The Winds of Fate"

Missionary casualties often occur in a vacuum of both poor soul-care and poor self-care. Missionaries notoriously bury themselves in their calling, and their work sometimes resembles more of a sarcophagus than a ministry.

Amazingly, very few missionary agencies discuss soul-care. It's a subject that generates little interest in the church, too. The subject is rarely broached.

Jesus asked, "Is there anything more important than your soul?"

Soul-care is a top priority for Jesus.

Maybe the idea of soul-care sounds a bit too mystical for some. Or, in the midst of modeling success formulas, plans, and policies our souls get lost in the planning, preparation, and performing.

I rarely raised the subject myself until I received my diagnosis of PTSD. This is a malady that a few well-meaning—"You need to love God more"—friends tried to tell me didn't exist. "There is no such thing as PTSD. You just need to stop thinking about yourself so much. Trust God more. Believe the Bible."

Post-Traumatic Stress Disorder redirected my soul. After diagnosis, therapy, and learning how to manage the affliction, my soul was on the mend. Psalm 23 became a precious passage of Scripture to me.

Missionary, your soul may someday feel like a fish out of water gasping for its aquatic breath. You'll need restoration. Elijah experienced this in his cave. Joseph in prison. Moses in the desert.

My valley of the shadow of death led me to search desperately for the greener pastures and still waters promised in David's famous twenty-third Psalm.

King David uttered what I believe are the four most important words in the Old Testament: "He restoreth my soul" (Psalm 23:3 KJV).

The twenty-third Psalm is a common passage of Scripture for people. It's mostly quoted at funerals. Interestingly, the twenty-third Psalm, which is often quoted in the King James Version, has very little to do with funerals. The ancient song speaks of the ingredients of a healthy soul.

I like to divide this Psalm into two main sections: soul-health and soul-living.

Soul-Health

The Lord is my shepherd; I shall not want.
He maketh me to lie down in green pastures:
he leadeth me beside the still waters.
He **restoreth my soul**: he leadeth me in the paths of righteousness for his name's sake. (Psalm 23:1-3 KJV, emphasis added)

Soul-Living

Yea, though I walk through the valley of the shadow of death, I will fear no evil: for thou art with me; thy rod and thy staff they comfort me.

Thou preparest a table before me in the presence of mine enemies: thou anointest my head with oil; my cup runneth over.

Surely goodness and mercy shall follow me all the days of my life: and I will dwell in the house of the Lord forever. (Psalm 23:4-6 KJV)

Shuwb is the Hebrew word translated in various English versions as "Restore, renew, revive or refresh." The Aramaic Bible in Plain English translates this word into the phrase, "brings back my soul."

The emphasis in the first three verses of Psalm 23 is about bringing one's soul back to health. You'll most likely discover that bringing back the missionary soul becomes vitally necessary in missionary work.

Restoration, health, revitalization, and preparation is the focus of this wonderful psalm.

King David authored this Psalm. His life was marked by many highs and lows. As a boy—maybe just fifteen years old—the simple shepherd boy was catapulted into hero status. His slaying of Goliath in the Valley of Elah turned him instantly into both a celebrity—and an enemy.

King Saul, who was initially grateful, then turned against David in resentment. He viewed David as a threat to his throne. In the limelight of praise and adulation, Saul betrayed David. So David began living as an outlaw. He experienced betrayal by his king, and Saul hunted him as a criminal. David experienced dire deprivation as he lived in the caves of Israel. Fifteen long years passed before David took his throne after being anointed king. But his rule was not immediately harmonious.

The war between Saul's house and David's throne lasted many years before David unified his rule. Imagine the impact of such strife upon David's soul.

Here in the twenty-third Psalm, David perhaps sat as Israel's king, looking back on his life. Dealing with the stresses of kingship marked a huge shift from his shepherd days. By far the wealthiest and most powerful man in the nation, he grappled with the struggles of ruling a small kingdom. Surrounded by enemies aimed at wiping out the new little nation pressured David immensely.

Perhaps he asked himself, "What is the one thing that kept me going all those days hiding in those caves? How did I survive all those valley battles?"

Through the betrayals, marital problems, strife, and personal failures, what is the one thing that restored David from his lows? David looked back on his days of shepherding in the fields of Judah, on the lessons he learned, and on his soul-restoration experiences in those green pastures with his sheep.

Soul-Fitness

In the first three verses, David spoke of a time of soul-restoration "Restore" here literally means "to bring back the soul." David sought to bring his soul back to a healthier place amid incredible, crushing lows. When your soul dries up, when you contemplate leaving the field, leaving the ministry, and maybe leaving the faith—where do you go?

David cried out: "Have mercy on me, Lord, for I am in distress. Tears blur my eyes. My body and soul are withering away" (Psalm 31:9). David's words cry out from the hearts of many today.

David looked to his Shepherd. For David, the soul—the real you— was the highest consideration. To cope with the stresses of life, the great king fixed his soul on four principles of health.

First - Connection with the Shepherd

"The Lord is my shepherd . . ." "Lord" here comes from the Hebrew word *râ'âh*, indicating many encouraging qualities of our shepherd. According to *Gesenius' Hebrew and Chaldee Lexicon*, the word "shepherd" means "to feed, shepherd, or tend to a flock. As far as the origin of the word, it probably carries a sense of **looking upon . . . with pleasure**" (emphasis added).[22]

David wrote: "My shepherd looks upon me with pleasure."[23] David's connection with the Great Shepherd brought him to a rich relationship of enjoyment. "The Lord is my shepherd; he takes great pleasure in me."

Think about this for a moment. When was the last time you thought, "God takes pleasure in me"?

Yes, David failed many times. So severe were his shortcomings that God radically stepped in to bring David back into his fold. Yet God's pleasure in David kept his soul connected to God.

Get this: Even in our downtimes—our soul doubts—God still finds reasons to take pleasure in his sheep! How do you feel about that, my sheepish friend?

Soul-health requires a connection to someone or something greater than one's self. Our soul is shepherd-dependent. Without a shepherd, one's soul wanders into dangerous valleys unaware and exposed.

Notice what David didn't say. He didn't say, "The Lord is *a* shepherd." Many people ascribe some value or worth to God in their lives. David cited God as more than just an addition. David's shepherd statement is practical, personal, and absolute. The shepherd was everything or nothing. Either a shepherd leads and a soul follows, or a soul wanders away to its own peril.

My forty years of missionary and pastoral work attests to the fact that many wandering souls call out to a shepherd for help that they are unwilling to follow. When faced with job loss, call out to the Shepherd. When suffering a horrible divorce, look to the Shepherd. Struggling with an addiction? Call out to God. When that phone call comes from the doctor about an illness, call, "Help me, Jesus." In the maladies of life, many turn to the Shepherd. But eventually they wander off again to unsafe pastures, into the clutches of the predator seeking to devour them.

Many years spent living among Zulu rural villagers in South Africa taught me that there is nothing more helpless than sheep. Apart from the watchful eye of a shepherd, harm always marks their end.

Whether in the high, cool, mountain air of Lesotho, Africa, or in the hot valleys of Natal, South Africa, sheep can't survive apart from their shepherd. Without their shepherd, they wander aimlessly into harm's way, clueless to their impending doom.

We also experience such enemies. Depression, anxiety, busyness, addiction, capacity, margin, strife, conflict, hatred, trauma, victimization, and a host of other adversaries seek to slay us in the dark caves of our human challenges. In my challenges and downtimes of life, confidence gains footing in my soul by the thought, "The Lord is my shepherd—taking pleasure in me . . ."

Second - Contentment in the Shepherd

David adds to his absolute statement of personal fact, "The Lord is my shepherd, I shall not want." Literally, "I do not lack" (Psalm 23:1 YLT). This is quite an incredible statement for a king looking back on his young shepherding years.

Surrounded by power, authority, wealth, and pleasure, David boiled his life down to one essence: "The Lord is my shepherd, in him, I have all I need." The caring shepherd is the dominant theme.

Sheep from different cultures thousands of years ago worried about the same stuff we do today. Look at just a few Bible verses reassuring us that a caring shepherd cares for his sheep:

Do not be afraid or discouraged, for the Lord will personally go ahead of you. He will be with you; he will neither fail you nor abandon you. (Deuteronomy 31:8)

Don't love money; be satisfied with what you have. For God has said, "I will never fail you. I will never abandon you." (Hebrews 13:5)

Commit everything you do to the Lord. Trust him, and he will help you. (Psalm 37:5)

And why worry about your clothing? Look at the lilies of the field and how they grow. They don't work or make their clothing, yet Solomon in all his glory was not dressed as beautifully as they are. And if God cares so wonderfully for wildflowers that are here today and thrown into the fire tomorrow, he will certainly care for you. (Matthew 6:28-30)

Don't worry about anything; instead, pray about everything. Tell God what you need, and thank him for all he has done. Then you will experience God's peace, which exceeds anything we can understand. His peace will guard your hearts and minds as you live in Christ Jesus. (Philippians 4:6-7)

Give all your worries and cares to God, for he cares about you. (1 Peter 5:7)

David directly linked his contentment to his Shepherd. He sourced meaning and significance to "the Existing One"—the Lord, his Shepherd (Psalm 1:1).[24] How did this king of Israel come to such a personal, confident relationship with God? God earned David's trust through his constant care for him.

Third - Care of the Shepherd

Get some rest. The Hebrew word for "Lie down" is *rabats* and is in the Hiphil stem. Some versions translate the phrase as "He lets me rest . . ." (NLT)

However, the verb stem points toward a causative, more forceful, "He makes me lie down..." (NASB). The shepherd forces his sheep to take necessary rest. Rest is the dire need of our day in our American culture.

"Forty-five percent of Americans say that poor or insufficient sleep affected their daily activities at least once in the past seven days," reported the National Sleep Foundation.[25]

In Brigid Schulte's book *Overwhelmed: Work, Love, and Play When No One Has the Time,* the author, a writer for *The Washington Post*, notes Americans' obsession with busyness. She writes:

> In the U.S., however, we have made a cult of busyness. Most of us limp by with just two weeks of vacation a year, and many of us don't even use that pitiful amount of time. We assign status based on who works the longest hours and gets the least sleep, even though other countries with 30-day vacations and limits on how long people can work have higher productivity rates.[26]

Cara Heissman, publisher of *Tiny Buddha*, draws a correlation between extreme busyness and stress. "Being crazy-busy implies stress; and our body can only take so much pressure before it activates its stress response and runs on 'survival or panic mode.'"[27]

Some of the most out-of-control people I know constantly flit about hyperventilating from one place to another under the veil of productivity. And missionaries are some of the busiest people I know.

The shepherd realized that his sheep needed rest. He forced his sheep to do what they naturally did not desire to do: rest.

Blessed with fifteen grandchildren, it's interesting for me to watch the battle for rest when their moms or dads announce bedtime. In my oldest son's home, bedtime occurs at the same time every evening. And almost every evening there is wailing, weeping, and cries of, "But I'm not tired!" But within just a few minutes of laying down, all fall fast asleep. Rest is forced because it's best for these little ones, even though they fight against it. It provides the parents a few hours of peace and rest.

When we don't rest well, it affects our moods and behavior. It negatively impacts a whole range of coping skills and cognitive abilities. Sleep-deprived people tend not to look their best either when they are running on empty all the time. Tired, baggy eyes tell sleep-deprived stories. Long-term sleep-deprivation tends to lead toward ill health, too.[28][29]

Getting quality rest is one of the best things you can do for yourself. Sitting in front of a blue screen hours a day does not aid in rest. EEG studies—which detect electrical activity in the brain—found that higher-functioning levels of the brain[30] go offline when we zombie out in front of media, smart phones, and computers.[31]

Find your special place. Have you ever laid down in a green pasture looking up at the sky? As the wind blows, the clouds pass, and the high grass covers the horizon, rest is found. Sheep, led by their shepherd, lay down in deep grass away from it all in a quiet place. When is the last time you sat by a quiet stream or in a quiet place? This is challenging to do in our busy world today, isn't it?

There's something special about still waters and green pastures. Explore. Find your quiet place. Schedule times for your quiet place to lay down in your green pastures. Make sure your quiet place is a place of tranquility rather than just another item on a to-do list of busyness.

During one of my pastorates, it was a great struggle to find rest. Living in a very rural area near the Canadian border, I took up photography at the urging of my oldest son.

Armed with a used Canon Rebel EOS camera and a set of decent lenses, almost every day off found me in the wilderness exploring nature photography. This became my resting place. My love for photography transformed me into a decent photographer, but most of all it provided mental decoupling and de-stressing.

Now that I'm often traveling again, stress presents many challenges. My son recently presented me with a couple of new lenses for my old Rebel camera. It was a hint. "Dad pick up your camera again. You need it."

Exhale. Thank you, son.

Restore your soul back to health. *Shuwb* or "restored" in verse three reminds us of the purpose of the shepherd: to restore soul-health. Our souls do not live in perpetual health and strength. Sheep who are under constant danger from the perils of nature's enemies need quiet and rest.

Again, understanding the verb stem here is helpful. *Shuwb* here is in the Polel stem, indicating "to lead away enticingly" to a repairing, refreshing place.[32] This wonderful word is also in the imperfect verb tense, indicating that restoration is an ongoing process of health and frequent repetition.[33] Spend time often with the Shepherd in your green pastures and beside your still waters.

Fourth - Confidence in the Shepherd

Sheep don't know their journey's end. We try to plan our lives, but much of the journey is unknowable until one arrives. "We can make our plans, but the Lord determines our steps" (Proverbs 16:9). Whatever one's level of planning, life is full of twists and turns. Confidence in the Shepherd acknowledges that our lives belong to one other than ourselves. The soul exists for a higher purpose.

David's confidence in his Shepherd focused on the Shepherd's purpose for his sheep rather than on a sheep's desire for itself. The Shepherd renews and guides a soul, bringing honor to the Shepherd's name (Psalm 23:3). The flock belongs to the Shepherd, and only he knows where to lead his sheep. David, arguably the most powerful man in the world at this time, saw both the beauty of the universe (Psalm 8:3), and the security of a shepherd. "How precious is your unfailing love, O God! All humanity finds shelter in the shadow of your wings" (Psalm 36:7).

Soul-Living

Healthy souls navigate life's trials prepared to meet its challenges. "Even when I walk through the darkest valley . . ." (Psalm 23:4).

What is the darkest valley you're facing? For me, my darkest valley led to a diagnosis of PTSD a few years ago. Years of helping AIDS orphan children and seeing horrible deaths and murders in South Africa took its toll.

Keeping an emotional distance from sick children proved to be impossible. The death of a little Zulu girl named Andiswa set my brain into a jumbled mess as I tried to cope with vivid images of suffering, brutality, and loss. My valley was deep, dark, and terrifying.

The Shepherd does not promise a ministry free from danger. The Shepherd promises to lead his missionary sheep through life's valleys of the shadow of death.

"I will not be afraid, for you are close beside me" (Psalms 23:4). God surrounded me with several shepherds. He prepared my way and set a table in the presence of my enemies.

Randy, a pastor friend, and his church valued my soul's health.

Brenda, director of Care Ministries, got me in touch with Tom, a Christian therapist.

Through the generous donations of members at Constance Free Church, all my expenses were covered.

Tom taught me how to manage the vivid images of brutality I had witnessed over my many years of serving in South Africa.

I learned not to fear what my brain struggled to comprehend. "Your rod and your staff protect and comfort me," became my mantra (Psalm 23:4).

Through the pain and struggle of reliving some awful stuff, comfort and new purpose appeared and healing began. In the presence of my enemies, God anointed my head with healing. Once again, my cup, my life, began to overflow with blessings (Psalm 23:5). I learned that God often brings many shepherds alongside us to help guide us through our valley of the shadow of death.

"You prepare a feast for me in the presence of my enemies (Psalm 23:5)." Enemies seek to rend sheep to bits. David fought many enemies, including the Philistines, Hittites, Moabites, Zobahites, Ammonites, Amalekites, and Edomites.

Other enemies sought his demise as well. Depression, sexual wanderings, bad decisions, pride, family strife, and traumatic losses afflicted David throughout his life.

David experienced life at the table with his enemies.

"Surely your goodness and unfailing love will pursue me all the days of my life . . ." (Psalm 23:6). I learned again that I can count on my Shepherd and the herdspeople he sends to help guide me through troubled valleys.

Souls that seek and follow their Shepherd can live in health and confidence even in the darkest of struggles. They're able to claim with confidence: "Trust in the Lord with all your heart; do not depend on your own understanding. Seek his will in all you do, and he will show you which path to take" (Proverbs 3:5-6).

For further soul-considerations get a copy of my book *Son Risings: Discovering and Caring for the Real You* (available on Amazon, Kindle, and KU Kindle Unlimited).

Considerations

1. What does the concept of soul-care mean to you?

2. How do you care for your soul?

3. What valleys are you experiencing right now?

4. What can you do to improve the health of your soul?

(10)

Your Mission's Agency

Meeting the In-Laws

Choosing a missions agency is like choosing a spouse. The in-laws almost always come with the deal. Some married couples get along well with their in-laws. Others find their in-laws are nosy, prying, distant, or cold.

Here's a secret. Sometimes the in-laws struggle with you, too. Managing your relationship with your agency is essential. Paying close attention to your agency's policies, practices, and procedures can determine your degree of contentment with them and theirs with you.

If your missions agency catered to just one missionary—you—then hundreds of changes might occur to suit you. Agencies however, exist to serve many missionaries.

Our agency, for example, serves over 700 missionaries. Policies, practices, and procedures are developed by a missions committee and implemented by the missions office staff for the benefit of all missionaries—not just one missionary. This necessitates a limiting of some desires for one to grant liberty to the group of missionaries as a whole.

There are literally hundreds of missionary agencies available for missionaries today. Choose your agency wisely. Your happiness—and the agency's office staff—will probably depend upon it.

Some of the advantages of going through a missionary agency are:

1. **Network** – Missionary agencies help provide a network that allows missionaries to raise funds more effectively.

2. **Resources** – Some agencies provide a host of beneficial resources.

3. **Training** – Other agencies provide excellent training.

4. **Legal Requirements** – Certain countries will not permit a missionary to enter their country without backing from a recognized agency.

    Many non-Western missionaries gain entrance into another country for missionary service through an agency that sponsors them in a particular country.

5. **Team Ministry** – Other agencies offer a variety of opportunities to serve on a team, from short-term mission trips to internships and career missions.

6. **Vision, Mission, and Momentum** – Agencies can possess great appeal due to their focus, recruiting, and momentum. While one allows much autonomy to missionaries, another may focus upon a single type of people group.

7. **Member Care** – Some agencies provide excellent member care for their overseas personnel. Here are just a few of many examples to consider:

    - What happens if you or a family member needs to be medevaced to the States for urgent medical care?
    - Who is behind you to assure you'll receive care if you get cancer?
    - What if you or a family member is kidnapped?
    - What happens if you suffer a spiritual challenge?
    - What happens if you need a loving pat on the back or a kick in the pants?

8. **Clearing of Missionary Funds** – For support-raising missionaries, missions agencies receive donations from a missionary's supporters and deposits them into the missionary's account. Usually a list of those donors is emailed to the missionary.

9. **Agency Assistance** – Agency assistance can include practical helps such as health insurance, saving for retirement, receipting donations, newsletters, forwarding mail, transportation for furloughs, and housing.

10. **Providing a network for association, fellowship, and raising of funds** – Our own agency provides wonderful opportunities to meet pastors and missionaries. It's valuable for this reason alone.

11. **Financial Security** – Some missionary agencies pay their missionaries. They receive a check via direct deposit like any

other employee. This eliminates the need to raise support or to self-fund missionary endeavors.

12. **Encouragement** – Having just returned from a wonderful missionary reunion reminds me that encouragement is a big factor in choosing your missions agency.

For a full week, while staying at a very nice hotel, Kathy and I listened to messages and testimonies from a dozen missionaries. Our leaders spoiled our missionaries spanning four generations.

However, we often find ourselves ministering to missionaries who are on the field without an association or missions agency. Some of the reasons for their decision to enter missionary service independently are:

1. **Cost.** Many agencies charge missionaries for their services. A missionary with whom I spoke recently mentioned her agency raised the amount taken from her support for office and administration fees from six percent to eight percent.

   One agency charges a flat fee of $7.50 per donation.

   I've heard of amounts as high as twenty percent of the missionary's gross financial support.

It costs money to process missionary funds. This is a business fact. Personnel, banking, and the structure necessary to process missionary funds costs. Someone has to pay for this expense.

My agency asks donors to pick up the cost for each missionary they support. Graciously, our churches agree to do so.

If the cost is not underwritten by someone, the missionary usually pays. This is simply the cost of doing business.

2. **Insurance**. Some require missionaries to enroll in their group insurance plan. This requirement is for the missionary's benefit, but often is an expense some missionaries are unwilling to incur.

Consider this. If, while on your field, you're diagnosed with cancer, where will you receive treatment? Most likely your home country of origin. For American missionaries, the United States is usually the best option.

One missionary argued, "I'm living in a country with free health coverage. If I get cancer, I can just go back to the United States and get insurance to cover my cancer." But insurance companies don't function in such a manner. If they did, they wouldn't survive financially.

Missionaries suffer much higher illness rates than normal Americans residing in the States. Consider this when making your decision.

3. **Inability to meet the standards of a missions agency's requirements**. Schooling, theological alignment, training, age, health, and other considerations make up an agency's minimum standards.

One missionary in his mid-thirties shared: "I'm not spending four years in college, a year of internship, and three years raising my support. I'm just going to get to the field."

4. **Their home church as a sending agency**. This is a growing trend. Some believe this model is more biblical.

5. **Flexibility**. Some missionaries feel going to the field independently allows them a greater ability to do what they believe aligns better with their calling. Rather than request permission and follow procedures, they can just do it. Alone, they are more mobile and nimbler to maneuver.

6. **The go-it-alone mentality**. Sometimes a missionary's mindset is: "God called me. I don't need anyone's help."

7. **Starting your own 501c3.** This is becoming more popular. I regularly meet missionaries who clear donor's funds through their own 501(c)(3) nonprofit organization. This requires careful consideration before embarking on such a course. There are many fiscal ramifications and tax compliances. Many missionaries simply don't possess the expertise to comply with IRS regulations.

This list is by no means exhaustive. Make sure you study well your agency of choice. Once on the field, many missionaries discover that they don't care for their in-laws and seek a divorce. Changing agencies is possible, but it's rarely easy. Some donors unwilling to make the crossover with you may drop your support.

One final word on this subject. Having met numerous missionaries during missionary field retreats one common thread emerges.

Missionaries sent through established mission agencies usually enjoy far greater financial support than their counterparts.

Regularly, we meet missionaries trying to survive so severely under supported that life and ministry barely ekes out an existence.

Missionary life is difficult enough without adding severe financial pressures to the mix. There is nothing unspiritual about raising enough financial support to provide for your family and ministry.

Considerations

1. How many agencies have you considered?

2. What are the strengths of your top agency consideration?

3. What are its weaknesses?

4. What are the pros and cons of either going through an agency or going to the field as an independent?

5. What do you bring to a missions agency to enhance its effectiveness?

(11)

Tame Your Dragon First

"It does not do to leave a live dragon out of your calculations, if you live near him."

Gandalf in *The Hobbit* by J. R. R. Tolkien

Missionary, tame your dragon before you leave for your field of service. If you don't, it may devour you once you're on the field.

Here's the thing. We all have chinks in our armor. When enough pressure is applied to these weak points, our missionary armor can—and often does—fail.

The stresses and challenges of a new place, people, and purpose brings to the surface the dross of our souls. As the writer of Hebrews says, "every weight that slows us down, especially the sin that so easily trips us up" (Hebrews 12:1).

What is the weight that slows you down? That sin that trips you up? Name it. This is your dragon.

Weaknesses, habits, shortcomings, personal deficits, sin-leanings, and other stuff that we keep hidden—I refer to this fallen reality as our dragons. Your dragon is that problem in your life about which

> What's your dragon?
> Your dragon is that thing trips you up continually.

you don't really want to talk. You know that thing you keep concealed, don't you?

The anxiety attacks you try to keep hidden.

The broken relationships with the family members you plan to leave behind once you arrive on your field.

Those dark moments in solitude you spend looking at your blue screen accessing . . . you know.

The relationship problems in your marriage that you hope the magic wand of missionary work will solve.

Those prescriptions you know you're taking too much of.

The occult exposure you experienced as a kid.

The trauma buried deep in your soul that wounded you as a child and now haunts you as an adult.

The anger you carry towards your father for not coming to a single football game. Especially the game when you scored four touchdowns against Holy Angels High School during your Homecoming in 1974.

Are we getting warm?

That explosive temper you think you keep hidden.

Your inability to get along well with others. There are quite a few out there in the missionary world.

Not ever feeling good enough to do something worthwhile.

You know that dragon. Your dragon. The thing that slays you. That habit that slows you down and trips you up. The weight that fatigues you.

Where's Your Dragon Hiding?

Dragons are not real, of course, but let's pretend they are for a few moments, and you will soon get the connection.

A dragon, when first acquired, is like most infant animals: They're cute. My step-dad once acquired a cute puppy that grew into a mammoth beast. The half-German Shepherd half-Doberman once ripped his custom van to shreds after he left the dog alone in the vehicle for only fifteen minutes. The dog did $6,000 worth of damage to his beloved vehicle.

In infancy, most animals appear to be great pets. Your dragon is like that, too. A young dragon is not that much trouble at first. It's easily kept hidden. It's so small you barely notice it. It understands your needs. A newly acquired dragon is always there for you. It heeds your every call. In fact, controllability is a major advantage of owning a young dragon.

A young dragon provides many benefits. They're mythical, or so it seems, taking you to fantasies never imagined. A dragon takes you on exciting voyages. Deep, dark, exotic places await you—places you didn't know existed. Your young dragon offers unconditional acceptance, too—at least in the beginning. And this little fellow will take you just about anywhere you want to go and whenever you want to go for as long as you want to stay.

Acceptance is a young dragon's greatest virtue. Your dragon accepts you just the way you are. There are no conditions. There are no responsibilities. You may present yourself any way you like. Whether in a bad mood or a bit grumpy, you're accepted. Are you happy and excited? Perfect! There's no nagging, no fault-finding, no conditions. Yes, you can just be you.

Your dragon can thrill you with its magical powers, beyond your wildest expectations. It's somewhat of a shape-shifter, too. Your dragon will be anything *you* want it to be. It appears in any form you conjure up. And it's so much more!

In the beginning, the cost of such a relationship is minimal. There is no cost commitment. Perhaps best of all, there are zero relational struggles and hassles.

It gives, expecting nothing in return—at least in the beginning. It's almost too good to be true. Yes, a young dragon seems perfect in every way. It's quite a wonder to behold.

Dragons are quite the rage these days. It seems everybody has one, two, or three of them. But then they start to grow. That's when the trouble starts. That's when the dragon begins to take control of your life, exacting an ever-increasing price for its services.[34]

Missionary, once you're living in your field of service, if you've not tamed your dragon, it will devour you and everyone near you. A new place, new culture, new language, and unfamiliar territory is not a good place to bring a wild, unruly dragon.

The mission field is the perfect place for your dragon to grow unhindered. Sin deficits, sinful practices, troubled family backgrounds, anxiety, weak marriages, family problems, depression, and many other struggles nurture a young dragon.

> Missionary, once you're living on your field of service, that dragon you've kept hidden will devour you.

Before you know it, your little companion becomes an eight-story tall fire-breathing menace devouring your world. Any secret little problem you're hiding or ignoring now will devour you once you're over there on your mission field.

Tame Your Marriage Dragon

Talking with a group of member care missionaries from a dozen different missions agencies, the topic of missionary marriages arose. Sadly, every single member care associate shared a plethora of stories of failed missionary marriages. Most of those had occurred within the past twelve months.

The most common scenario resulted in a missionary spouse hooking up with a national on the field. The cheating spouse then served divorce papers and abandoned the marriage and children.

A usual pattern of behavior included manipulation of the departing spouse over the abandoned spouse.

He left because she didn't respect him.

She left because he didn't love her.

He left because she didn't meet his needs.

She left because there was no romance.

It's tragic and amazing to listen to the lists of grievances the cheating spouse often levels upon an abandoned spouse to justify their reasons for adultery, betrayal, and abuse.

Remember, these are missionaries we are talking about.

Missionary divorces don't make up the majority of our interactions with missionaries—not even close. Missionary divorces do occur frequently enough, however, that I am compelled to mention it here.

This past year alone, Kathy and I spoke with four missionary wives whose husbands divorced them for younger local women from the countries in which they lived. Each husband sported long-term, habitual exposures to pornography.

Please hear this: If your marriage isn't healthy, strong, and vibrant—then please don't become a missionary. Not yet. Strengthen your marriage first. Becoming a missionary does not fix a marriage.

You don't belong out there if your marriage is not strong. I didn't write the rules of spiritual leadership. God did. (See Ephesians 5, Titus 3, and 1 Timothy 3.)

Don't be guilty of King David's sin, which ended Uriah and Bathsheba's marriage—not to mention Uriah's life—and gave the enemies of God cause to blaspheme the Lord (1 Kings 15:5 and 2 Samuel 12:14 KJV).

Here is a list of some great resources to help you with your marriage:

Healing Your Marriage When Trust is Broken: Finding Forgiveness and Restoration by Cindy Beall

Rebuilding a Marriage Better Than New by Cindy Beall

The Emotionally Destructive Marriage: How to Find Your Voice and Reclaim Your Hope by Leslie Vernick

For Women Only, Revised and Updated Edition: What You Need to Know about the Inner Lives of Men by Shaunti Feldhan

Marriage On The Rock: God's Design For Your Dream Marriage by Jimmy Evans

Lifelong Love Affair: How to Have a Passionate and Deeply Rewarding Marriage by Jimmy Evans

Strengths Based Marriage: Build a Stronger Relationship by Understanding Each Other's Gifts—by Jimmy Evans and Allan Kelsey

His Needs, Her Needs: Building an Affair-Proof Marriage by Willard F Harley, Jr.

The Marriage Builder: Creating True Oneness to Transform Your Marriage—by Larry Crabb

"Everything You Should Know Before You Get a Divorce" by Keith Green[35]

When I suggested one of the above resources, a missionary once proclaimed, "I don't have time to do all that reading." My reply sought to push him into thought. "What do you have time to do? Work on your ministry, or your marriage? How much ministry do you gain if you lose your marriage?" He looked at me with a blank stare. I asked another question: "Of the two, which would end your ministry if you lose it? Losing your marriage, or losing the church you're currently working in?"

Missionary, take time to build your marriage. If you can't shape a decent marriage, what makes you capable of building an effective ministry as a missionary?

Slay Your Porn Dragon

In this modern day of computers, smartphones, and media, pornography is easily accessible. You must get control of this dragon and eliminate it quickly before it slays you. And, my friend, that's exactly what pornography does: slays you. It slays your intimacy, your relationships, your spouse, your marriage, your family, your integrity, and your future. I've seen it a hundred times, even among missionaries.

The porn dragon desires to turn you into a pervert. It ruins marriage, families, and reduces men—in particular—to their lowest levels of deprivation.

Harry Schaumburg is a speaker, author, and counselor specializing in the area of sexual sin in the church. He has said:

"Several years ago, a seminary professor told me, 'We no longer ask our entering students if they are struggling with pornography; we assume every student is struggling. The question we ask is, "How serious is the struggle?"' One missions agency told me that 80% of their applicants voluntarily indicate a struggle with pornography, resulting in staff shortages on the field."[36]

If you're struggling with pornography, I've written a book that offers a five-step way to gain control of its clutches: *Boundaries: 5 Steps to Getting Your Life Back* (available at Amazon and on Kindle).

For addictions and anxieties in general, I've put together a workbook: *Get Your Life Back Addiction Workbook* (available at Amazon, Barnes and Noble, and on Kindle).

If you feel uncomfortable with the title including the word "Addiction," then pick up a copy of *Get Your Life Back!: Journal.* This is the same workbook, but with a different name. All are available at Amazon and on Kindle.

Again, if you struggle with pornography, don't go to the field until you've:

Established sound **boundaries**.

Implemented ironclad **accountability**.

Learned to regularly biblically **confess** your sin.

Gained **knowledge** of the dreadful consequences of porn.

Acquired godly **sorrow** about your sin (2 Corinthians 7:10).

Your Dragon of Past Issues

In my book *To Hell, Back, and Beyond– A PTSD Journey: When Faith and Trauma Collide,* I share how the traumatic injuries of childhood accompanied me to South Africa. Undiscussed and ignored, events of my past returned to haunt me once I was exposed to the extreme suffering of Zulu children in KwaZulu Natal, South Africa.

If an injury is part of your past, please get help to heal and to learn how to manage your trauma. Situations on the field can cause your trauma to resurface in the most damaging of ways.

Where's Your Dragon Now?

Personality traits. Conflict. A critical spirit. Isolation. What is your biggest struggle right now? Most likely, it will become a bigger issue on the field unless you get your dragon under control now.

Become familiar with the chinks—the soft spots—in your personal armor. Know your weaknesses and learn to manage them. For example, when one fails to manage their anger, that anger taints relationships, family, and life on the field. A sin leaning towards pornography ends enough missionary ministries that I feel compelled to mention this again.

> The mission field isn't a magic wand to rectify our problems. It often increases our malfunctions. It does not end them.

If you suffer from anxiety, get help learning how to deal with this before leaving for the field. On the field such issues magnify themselves.

Deal with your deficits now. On the field, in high-stress environments, your dragon will gain momentum if not disciplined. Think about it. You'll be surrounded by new people. Learning a new language. Possibly working with a missionary you don't like. Adjustments, adjustments and still more adjustments can power up the dragon.

Taming Your Dragon according to Paul

The apostle Paul spoke sound words concerning our efforts to tame our dragons. He wrote: "I discipline my body like an athlete, training it to do what it should. Otherwise, I fear that after preaching to others I myself might be disqualified" (1 Corinthians 9:27).

Considerations

1. Name your dragon. My greatest struggle is _____.

2. Who have you talked with about your dragon?

3. On a scale of one to ten—ten indicating complete victory—how well do you manage your dragon?

4. What's your plan to manage your dragon?

(12)

Show Me the Money!

"God's work done in God's way will
never lack God's supply."

Hudson Taylor

One of the couples from a church I pastored in Minnesota, enlisted for missionary service with a very respected agency. I was shocked at the amount of monthly support the agency required them to raise. Thirty months later they departed to their field fully supported.

Another young couple from the same church went through a different organization. Their monthly financial support goal seemed just as daunting. This couple was not nearly as effervescent as the first couple. Yet, in thirty months they raised their entire support.

Another young missionary couple raised most of their support over Facebook. Incredible.

There are many great resources that give instructions on support and fundraising. Some agencies provide excellent coaching for young missionaries. My purpose is not to discuss that which is so readily and expertly available today for missionaries who are raising support. In all our support-raising over the years, several principles come to mind for consideration.

God Promises to Provide for All Your Needs

Sometimes missionaries develop a mindset that, "Because I'm going to serve as a missionary, my family, friends, acquaintances, and church owe me financial homage." Oh, we're not that egregious, but numerous pastors and financial contributors share this perspective of fundraising missionaries. Often pastors share, "It's almost as if that missionary thinks I owe them support."

Let us understand one vital principle:

> No one owes you anything except God,
> who promises to provide for your needs.

Our support comes from God alone. Yes, the creator of the universe uses people to accomplish this purpose. God alone, however, has promised to supply for our every need. "And this same God who takes care of me will supply all your needs from his glorious riches, which have been given to us in Christ Jesus" (Philippians 4:19).

> No one owes a missionary anything except God who promises to meet your needs.

Avoiding becoming disappointed, bitter, and angry with people who do not follow through on their promises to send funds often becomes a major obstacle. This is a common issue with support-raising missionaries. Bitterness and resentment enter into their souls when prospective supporters don't respond or don't follow through on their promises to send monthly financial support.

Once I as sat at my favorite coffee shop in South Africa—Wimpy's—whimpering and complaining about a good many things to my sweet Kathy, I felt an uncomfortable presence off to my right side. Looking up, a young, well-dressed, professional Indian man stood there just looking at me.

Without introduction, he pointed his finger at me and said, "Sir, you remember this . . . The Scriptures say, 'My God will never leave thee or forsake thee!'" I looked down and replied, "Yes, you are correct." Looking back up, there was no one standing next to me. He must have walked out the door—or maybe there was another explanation? "Don't forget to show hospitality to strangers, for some who have done this have entertained angels without knowing it!" (Hebrews 13:2).

Bank on God first and foremost. You'll never beg for bread on your field of service (Psalm 37:25).

God Sources Missionary Support through People

It's continually amazes me how God touches people to supply the needs our lives and ministries. Support sometimes arrives from the most unique sources—like the ravens that fed Elijah.

This is our second time to launch out into the waters of deputation and financial support-raising. The first time, I was in my mid-twenties. Today, I'm in my sixties. I do not possess the pace or energy to cover the distances and churches young missionaries do today to raise their support. Our support is slowly coming in, in the most unusual, unsuspected ways.

I type these very words while watching three Chinese geese from the porch of a beautiful home just in front on the waters of Lake Granbury. This is a home—Shepherd's Missionary House—to help missionaries recover from the rigors of missionary service on difficult fields.

This is a fully furnished rent-free home provided by people we didn't know until two years ago.

God does indeed supply.

When we first began deputation—for the second time—I was skeptical. Would we be able to this again? I remember sharing that concern with our mission's director, Jon. I asked, "Jon, how am I going to raise our support again?" He looked at me and smiled.

The first church we visited provided me with a much-needed faith-correction. We shared our ministry in a very small church with a new pastor. There was no chance at gaining monthly financial support; this was what our guts told us as we entered the building that Sunday morning.

We shared our hearts with a group of about thirty people. After the service, the pastor gave me a much-appreciated, modest love offering.

As Kathy and I packed up our display and got in the car to leave, she said, "A man in the church gave me this." She pulled out eight $100 bills. After that Sunday, I stopped doubting. Thank you, God, for your loving, faith-correcting lessons.

If God opened a rock in the desert, forcing water to gush forth, he can source his provision to flow through his people during your dry seasons.

If God caused a donkey to talk to a wayward prophet, he can deliver just what you need when you need it.

If God caused a guy in the desert with a big stick to part the Red Sea, he can part your soul-doubts, bringing you to your promised land.

If God caused the sun to stand still to give extra light so that Joshua finished his conquest of the Amorites, he can supply both your needs and desires in him and through him.

God will do it, because he said he would do it! So, missionary, put your faith in God that he will do it!

Beware of the Idol of "My Support"

The nature of constant fundraising can cause us to look away from God. It's easy to do. I've done it many times myself over the years. It's natural to focus on a lack of financial support or a need for more support. When we focus more on our needs and less on our Provider, well . . . that's idolatry. Isn't it? Putting a thing above our focus upon our God.

Some missionaries are great fundraisers but poor missionaries. Others are great missionaries but poor fundraisers. Both extremes can tend to encourage too much emphasis on money: either the lack of it or a continual wanting for more.

What if I lose my support? Interestingly, missionaries often cite their fear of losing their support when they need to make difficult decisions.

What if supporters find out we have marriage problems? They'll drop my support.

What if my home church hears that one of our teenage daughters is cutting? They'll drop my support.

What if churches knew I'm struggling with an issue? What will they think of me? I'll lose my support.

What if a major contributor found out I struggle with budgeting and finances? I'll lose my support.

What if my churches knew I struggled with PTSD? What if they found out?

What if I have an eating disorder?

What if they knew my spouse hasn't left our house one time in the last three years?

What if...? *I'd lose my support!*

See where the emphasis is here? It's anywhere other than upon the God we claim to love and serve.

When support becomes a graven image. Anything that becomes a first consideration above God, Scripture calls an idol. Your support becomes an idol when it takes higher precedence than God in your life.

What if getting the help you need cost you ten percent of your support, or twenty or thirty percent of your finances? Would not that cost be worth dealing with your problem to become a healthier and holier servant of God?

Jesus encouraged, "Seek the Kingdom of God above all else, and live righteously, and he will give you everything you need" (Matthew 6:33).

It's really not your support anyway. David reminds us: "The earth is the Lord's, and everything in it. The world and all its people belong to him" (Psalm 24:1).

Support is God's provision, entrusting you to steward soundly that which he provides for faith, family, and ministry.

Keep your focus upon God, and he will keep his blessings upon you. A verse that God continually reinforces to me is Hebrews 11:6.

> And it is impossible to please God without **faith**. Anyone who wants to come to him must **believe** that God exists and that he rewards those who sincerely **seek** him. (emphasis added)

Three key essentials:

1. **Faith** – Acting upon that which you can't possibly figure out for yourself. Abraham leaving Ur of the Chaldees is a good example. It's not faith if you can do it all by yourself.

2. **Believe** – Is the actual acting upon faith. Both "faith" and "believe" are from the same Greek words. Faith is the noun, and believe is the verb. Faith is not faith unless one acts upon it—believes. Faith demands action.

3. **Seek** – Ready for the ride of your life? Do you really want to live on faith's edge and be part of God doing great stuff in your life? Then diligently seek God with your whole being and get ready for his rewards to pour upon you.

Considerations

1. What are your thoughts about raising your support?

2. How much financial support do you need to accomplish God's calling in your life?

3. Your support or God's provision? What are your thoughts here?

4. How will you please God by your faith?

5. How can you seek him diligently?

6. How much is enough?

(13)

Viewing God's Resources

"Do you not know that God entrusted you with that money (all above what buys necessities for your families) to feed the hungry, to clothe the naked, to help the stranger, the widow, the fatherless; and, indeed, as far as it will go, to relieve the wants of all mankind? How can you, how dare you, defraud the Lord, by applying it to any other purpose?"

"You have one business on earth—to save souls."

John Wesley

It's important to understand that we ask people to financially sacrifice for us so that we can fulfill our calling. We ask others to do with less so that we might do more. If your funds come from a mission board such as the IMB, those funds originated from the pockets of sincere donors. It's blood money coming from the sweat and the brows of people doing with less so that the missionary can accomplish more.

When I pastored in Minnesota, faithful giving members often shared their frustrations with missionaries in this area. One church member said, "Pastor, I could buy a much better car if I didn't give to missions."

Another senior living on limited income said, "Pastor, I can only afford to give twenty dollars a month to missions." Visiting with this faithful member in her subsistence-living apartment humbled me immensely.

In 2012, I stood by the bedside of an elderly lady in a nursing home up in Grand Rapids, Minnesota. She was a retired teacher in her nineties. In the 1950s, she taught forty school children ranging from first through sixth grade in a one-room school-house up on the Iron Range in northern Minnesota. I was there when she took her last breath.

> The money you receive comes from people who do with less so that you, the missionary, can accomplish more.

She lived a very frugal life. Her home was old, small, and not worth more than sixty thousand dollars. Yet she left a substantial amount of money in her will to support missionaries. She was one of our best givers. She out-gave many wealthy people in our church.

Here's the point: The money you receive for your family, ministry, and livelihood comes from people who do with less so that you—the missionary—can accomplish more.

In the missions organization where I am privileged to serve, one of our single missionary women served for decades in a third world county. She lived a life of poverty with impoverished people, serving the people she loved. She was ushered into heaven at the hands of an assassin.

It was surprising to learn that over the years she spent little of her financial support. By accumulating funds over the years, she left a substantial amount of money in her will toward helping missionaries equip themselves for their first arrival on their fields. She gave so that other missionaries might purchase that which she never possessed.

Do You Really Need That?

Yes, I'm walking on thin ice here. But not without good cause.

Before you purchase that new car, truck, office equipment, or expensive piece of property, please consider whether you truly need it.

Having served with Chief Scott in the Eagan Fire Department in Eagan, Minnesota, taught me much about prioritizing and purchasing.

While other departments in the Twin Cities purchased huge, expensive SUVs as their chief's vehicle, Chief Scott purchased a new, outfitted Ford Escape. The vehicle accomplished every task the bigger SUVs did, but with far less cost. And it improved the perception of the residents of Eagan toward the department.

Spend a season of prayer before buying that thing you believe you so desperately need. Few expect the missionary to live in poverty, but sensitivity toward donors is appreciated. It's also a very strategic practice if you're going to maintain your support and raise more.

During our many years in South Africa, the heat in the summer—and the cold in the winter—presented continual challenges. Many missionaries bought homes with in-ground swimming pools. I understand: It's hot in South Africa in the summer! It's not uncommon to see in-ground swimming pools.

Once an American pastor visiting one of the missionaries his church supported commented, "Not one person in my church owns a swimming pool." I thought about this for quite a while before coming up with an acceptable solution to avoid similar criticisms.

Installing split-level air conditioners in our home cost—at the time—about the same as putting in a small, in-ground pool. No donor would ever question such an expense, as most living in the United

States enjoys air conditioners. This was a wise move, and we never encountered a problem.

And, by luck, all our South African friends possessed in-ground swimming pools. Coincidence or strategic decision making? You be the judge.

Credit Card Debt—Burning $100 Bills

Years ago, I sat with a missionary who experienced extreme financial difficulty. That missionary is no longer with us.

He stated several times during our conversation, "I need to raise more support." The missionary enjoyed above-average financial support at that time. When we looked at his finances, it revealed the missionary's problem. That missionary didn't struggle with support; he struggled with spending.

The missionary carried over $40,000 of high-interest debt on nine credit cards. He asked, "What should I do?" He was paying off two percent per month, which at that time was the minimum payment by law. He was making a dollar per month minimum payment, which meant it would take fourteen years to pay off his credit cards—and that assumed the missionary didn't charge anything else on his credit cards. As his debt accumulated, so did his efforts to raise more support.

I offered him a solution: Resign as a missionary, get a secular job, and pay off the credit cards. Then enroll in a program to learn how to manage money. Then, and only then, reapply for missionary service. Stop wasting the sacrifices of God's people upon frivolous spending.

Missionary, please don't waste the hard-earned sacrificial money supporters give to you on thirty percent credit card interest fees.

The support we receive is often from seniors on fixed incomes, struggling young families, sacrificing church members, and others who could buy more if they gave less.

Let's go back and look at that missionary's $40,000 of credit card debt. The minimum interest payments currently on that amount is four percent in the United States as set by federal law. Four percent is $1,600 per month just to service the debt on those credit cards.

Now, share this with prospective supporters: "As part of our budgeting process, we intend to spend $1,600 per month of your contributions servicing the debt on our credit card borrowing." You would do better to burn one hundred-dollar bills than carry credit card debt.

Why give to banks that which God entrusts to you through his people for your ministry?

Purchase Your Vehicles, but . . .

Do you really need to ship a car to your field? Or can you purchase a vehicle on your field cheaper? The problem with shipping an automobile is that it often doubles the expense of the vehicle by the time you land it in the country and pay the taxes.

> "There are two questions a steward needs to consider.
> Who owns it?
> How much is enough?"
> Ron Blue

What happens when you break a window or need a part? Often you'll need to order it from the United States at far greater cost and time.

For some missionaries, shipping a vehicle is their only option. What is your best option to get the vehicle you need?

Save for Retirement, but . . .

Yes, save for retirement. Builder and boomer missionaries did not possess the financial vehicles available today in which to save for retirement. Many older, early missionaries retired in poverty. This is to our shame.

Today's missionaries can save for retirement quite easily. They will enjoy much better financial support in their elder years than past generations. Be wise in your retirement savings. Look at the costs of the products you use to invest your retirement.

Please, Take a Vacation, but . . .

Take a vacation. *Regularly*. Occasionally treat yourself to nice things. Be sensitive to your donors. If all a donor sees on your Facebook and Instagram are photos of beaches, parks, game reserves, baseball stadiums, Disneyland, Sea World, and other places they themselves can never visit, what are they supposed to think?

One young family in the church I pastored stated: "We should become missionaries. Then we can visit all those places, too." Perception is sometimes everything.

I suggest missionaries hold two Facebook and Instagram accounts. One for family and friends and the other for ministry. Share all your fun family stuff with friends and family. Share your ministry activities with supporters.

Proper View of Money?

What am I asking you to consider? Life is tough enough on the field without living like paupers. No one asks or expects this from the missionary. Few supporters want their missionaries to struggle financially. When good financial support starts coming in—and it will—, please consider your spending habits. Consider those who support you. And, most of all, remember: "Keep your life free from love of money, and be content with what you have, for he has said, 'I will never leave you nor forsake you'" (Hebrews 13:5 ESV).

Considerations

1. What does your budget look like?

2. How do you use a budget?

3. Describe your spending habits.

4. How does the way you handle money reflect the lordship of Jesus Christ in your life?

5. How does the manner in which you handle your donations reflect gratitude toward your donors?

(14)

Language or Languish

"If you talk to a man in a language he understands, that goes to his head. If you talk to him in his own language, that goes to his heart."

Nelson Mandela

Nelson Mandela's mother tongue was Xhosa. It's the second most spoken Bantu language in South Africa. He learned English in a missionary school as a young boy. After he was sentenced to prison, he learned to speak fluent Afrikaans, the language of his oppressors. He could also speak Zulu, and a few other languages, too.

In 1994, South Africa was on the brink of a civil war that pitted the sufferers of apartheid against whites. On the day of his presidential inauguration (May 10, 1994), I listened to Mandela with amazement as he calmed the nation in multiple languages.

Speaking Xhosa, Afrikaans, English, and some Zulu, he moved the nation toward peace instead of war. It's my personal belief that, at that moment, Nelson Mandela single-handedly prevented a bloodbath in South Africa.

A missionary once asked me to be the guest speaker at one of his Zulu churches. It was a pleasure to do so. I spoke to that Zulu congregation in Zulu without the help of a translator. Later that day, my missionary friend commented, "You had more affinity with my people in one sermon than do I after fifteen years of serving them through a translator."

Many missionaries rely almost solely upon translators. Yet the best way to connect with people is to learn to speak their language with a high level of fluency. Learn to speak their language, and you will sing the music of their hearts.

> Learn to speak their language, and you will sing the music of their hearts.

Language More Important than Doing

One's first inclination when arriving on the field is to get busy. Get to work! Do stuff! But you should resist that temptation. Whoa! Slow down! Make learning the language your highest priority in your first few years.

Enroll in language school. If you're fortunate enough to have access to a language school, *enroll*! Two years of full-time language study is not a waste. Becoming proficient in the local language will pay great dividends in the long run.

Hire a tutor. When we arrived in South Africa, there were no language schools to learn Zulu. South Africa is a country with eleven official languages and many more spoken dialects. Hiring a tutor was the first step for us. Often, missionaries meet with a tutor two or three times a week. Hire two tutors if necessary, and study the language every day. Make acquiring your new language a top priority.

Enroll in a language class. Kathy and I enrolled in a night class for Indian South Africans who were trying to learn the language. The class proved very helpful until they informed us that under the laws of the apartheid government at the time, we could no longer attend the class due to our skin color.

Enroll in a university. Although very challenging, studying Zulu with the University of South Africa (UNISA) proved extremely helpful. The test and study schedules provided structure and kept me disciplined.

Utilize apps. Today a myriad of apps provide language aids as never before. Looking in the app store today, over a dozen programs exist for learning the Zulu language. Devour them all!

Play with the kids! Children are wonderful language teachers. I used to ask Zulu children, "Yini le?" or, "What is this?" They thought it was a game. I'd regularly ask 100 questions of Zulu children as they giggled and laughed. "What is this? What is that?"

Watch TV and listen to the radio. Listening to Zulu radio and watching TV helped with flow and listening skills. Before you consider turning to a channel that speaks your language, why not spend an hour or two listening to your new language?

Read the newspaper. Often, I'd read the *iLanga* Zulu newspaper in South Africa while eating breakfast at my favorite coffee shop. Now I can read a copy on my smartphone. Gobble up everything you can read in your new language.

Seek Mastery over Mediocrity

Stay with it! The landscape is littered with missionaries who gave up after learning just enough to get by. I know this sounds harsh, but if I could do it all over again I'd spend more time mastering the Zulu language.

My level of Zulu was better than most missionaries. Looking back, though, I suspect it was not good enough.

One elder missionary serving in South Korea studied the language every morning, except Sunday, until the day he died. At the age of 84, he still studied the Korean language every morning.

Laugh at Yourself

You'll need to learn to laugh at yourself as you learn a new language. Most likely you'll make horrendous gaffes and blunders.

It was Easter Sunday morning in the Zulu township of Ezakheni outside Ladysmith, South Africa. After two years of language study with my tutor, Simon Dube, I could still barely carry on a conversation in the Zulu language.

That Easter Sunday, as I was speaking to a packed house and was well into the resurrection, a young Zulu mother with twin girls entered the building. They seemingly mesmerized the congregation. For one single moment, three hundred people gazed at this beautiful, young mother and her two five-year-old twin girls.

The two little girls wore beautiful, pink Easter dresses. With bonnets, white gloves, white stockings, and brand-new shoes, their cuteness captured the room. Believing the little girls' outstanding beauty deserved a public comment, I made my first mistake.

The second mistake occurred when I spoke. What I attempted to say was, "Mama, **ama<u>w</u>ele** akho avele kahle kimi kahlulu."

Or, "Madam, your twin girls are very beautiful to me indeed."

What I actually said was, "Mama, **ama<u>b</u>ele** akho avele kahle kimi kahlulu."

Or, "Madam, your breasts are very beautiful to me indeed."

The entire congregation smirked and giggled. My sweet wife, Kathy, roared with laughter from the back of the building. The most embarrassing part of the day soon followed.

In front of the entire church, the dear Zulu mother replied, "Uxolo fundis, lenza iphuta elikhulu kahulu." Or, "Excuse me, pastor, you've made a very grievous error."

With that she placed each hand on the head of her two little girls standing on both sides of her. She instructed, "Lawa amawele," or, "These are twins."

Then she reached up and squeezed both her breasts declaring, "Lawa amabele," or, "These are breasts."

Then she asserted, "Musa ukuphinda leliphuta futhi." This meant, "You mustn't make that mistake again."

I was absolutely embarrassed. I never repeated that error.

This, my friend, is not the worst of my mistakes. To share my most egregious Zulu vernacular errors, this book would carry an "R" rating for obscene language. Language acquisition is difficult and takes tenacity, discipline, and self-effacement.

Laughter is not an insult. In most cases, the laughter of a national when you make a mistake in their language is a gesture of endearment. Learn to laugh with them. Learn to laugh at yourself. Apologize for an error if necessary.

Engender an attitude of receiving correction. It's better they laugh acknowledging your mistakes than not alerting you to your errors. Sometimes

> If you can't communicate effectively, you can't connect deeply.

missionaries show frustration and irritation when a citizen offers correction. This is a sure way to guarantee you'll continue to make errors. Remember, if you can't communicate effectively, you can't connect deeply.

I once preached a message entitled, "What's in Your Pocket?" Since Zulu people often speak metaphorically, I thought it a great idea. However, I made a slight mistake in the message title, "Yini E**si**khukhuweni Sakho?" Now, "ekhukhwini" means "in the pocket." However, by adding those two little letters, "si," the meaning turned severely. Instead of "What's in Your Pocket?", the message title read, "What Afflicts Your Diseased, Swollen Testicle?"

No one offered a correction. Under the oppressive apartheid government system, a black person correcting a white man—especially publicly—was unacceptable.

Weeks later a Zulu man asked about another one of my messages. He said, "What was that all about, those sheep lost in a dress? I didn't understand." My reply was, "What dress?"

He continued, "Yes, you said that the sheep were lost in a dress." The word for "in a dress" in Zulu is "elokweni," but I was trying to talk about sheep lost in a hole ("emgodini"). My entire message centered upon a group of sheep lost in a dress!

After that moment, I encouraged my Zulu pastors to offer any corrections, and I promised them that I'd grow in grace to receive such corrections. They need not fear coming to me—a white man—to help me in their language.

Not encouraging and accepting of correction from national people? Well, let me share another gaffe, this one from a Catholic missionary.

I went to a Zulu funeral of a dignitary who had died in a car accident. The European priest conducting the ceremony repeatedly made the same grievous error.

What he meant to say as he pointed to the deceased in the closed casket was, "Um**q**onodo walendoda", or, "the mind of this man will rise again on the last day." Or, literally, "This man will rise again."

Unable to make the palatal click of the "q," he substituted it with an easier to pronounce dental consonant. The English voice dental fricative "th" completely changed the meaning of the word.

"What he repeatedly said was, "Um**th**ondo walendoda," or "the genital of this man will someday. . ." Well, you get the point.
There is a lot of difference between the click of a "p" and the sound of a "th." Two letters make a lot of difference. It's the same in English. **Th**ink, **s**tink, **w**ink, **bl**ink, **z**inc or ink. Get the point?

After the service, I spoke with several Zulu men from that church. Their reply to the mistakes made during the service was, "You can't tell that man, the priest, anything. He won't accept our instruction."

The Bible speaks of this ancient problem. "Those who refuse correction hate themselves, but those who accept correction gain understanding" (Proverbs 15:32 NCV).

Don't Leave Your Spouse Behind

This was the greatest mistake made in our missionary ministry. There were no full-time Zulu language schools to enroll in to master the basics of the language in a year or two. Much of my language acquisition took place with a private tutor in our home late at night as Kathy prepared the boys for bed. Sometimes it occurred out in Zulu villages and towns. Often Kathy stayed at home with our sons.

As a result, Kathy never became fluent in the language. Most of this was due to my visionary, charge forward, master and conquer way of thinking.

Whatever method you use to learn the language of the people you're serving, **don't leave each other behind!**

Women Often Acquire the Language Quicker

Women often grasp and speak the language quicker and better than do their husbands. Perhaps this is true because of men's fix-it approach to much of life. Women seem to let the language speak to them. Men seem to speak to the language, telling it what it must do. Women listen. Men command.

Women are more relational. They love to visit, talk, and share. They possess an intuition that allows them to absorb language rather than try to conquer it. The language becomes their friend. To men, the language is often a foe.

Once, while struggling with Zulu, a Wycliffe missionary who specialized in linguistics and translation said to me: "Don, let the language speak to you. Stop trying to speak to it. Let Zulu master you rather than you trying to master Zulu." These proved good words. Following her advice made my Zulu surge forward into fluency.

Listen to Your Kids

Your children, if immersed, will acquire the language and speak it as fluently as mother-tongue speakers. Learn to listen to them. Ask them to correct your errors.

My son, Donnie, speaks Afrikaans with a South African accent. I focused primarily on the Zulu language, so my ability in Afrikaans is minimal. Donnie regularly corrects my attempts in the language.

Be a learner. Be humble enough to receive instruction and correction. Never stop learning the language of the people you serve.

Language or Languish

In every case, every missionary void of fluency in the language of the people they serve struggle to connect. They stumble to understand what is taking place in their ministry before their very eyes. Stunted relationships, frustrations, and misunderstandings dominate their interactions with national people.

Missionary, if you say you care, then show it. Take the time to master the language of the people. It's a true way into their hearts. Only then will your message be heard.

> They were completely amazed. "How can this be?" they exclaimed. "These people are all from Galilee, and yet we hear them speaking in our own native languages!
>
> Here we are—Parthians, Medes, Elamites, people from Mesopotamia, Judea, Cappadocia, Pontus, the province of Asia,
>
> Phrygia, Pamphylia, Egypt, and the areas of Libya around Cyrene, visitors from Rome
>
> (both Jews and converts to Judaism), Cretans, and Arabs. And we all hear these people speaking in our own languages about the wonderful things God has done!"
>
> They stood there amazed and perplexed. (Acts 2:7-12)

Considerations

1. What's your plan to learn the language?

2. What level of language acquisition do you wish to achieve?

3. How long do you think it will take to master the language?

4. How correctable are you?

(15)

Aim High, but Aim Straight

"Life is what happens to us while
we are making other plans."

Allen Saunders

I sat in a Sunday service at a megachurch of a well-respected, accomplished pastor in the deep South. During his message, he discussed missionary evangelism. Having just attended a large conference of his denomination on "The Future of Missionary Work," he stated his alarm at a statement made at the conference.

The speaker at the conference stated, "What we really do is send our missionaries out with the hope that after thirty years they build solid enough relationships with the national people so that they can share the gospel."

The pastor exclaimed in astonishment to his congregation that Sunday morning, "You've got to be kidding me!"

He went on to gently denounce the statement, explaining that he could travel anywhere in the world, hire a translator, and tell people about Jesus from the first moment he stepped on the "foreign field."

He continued, "I confidently asserted that our missionaries need to establish some goals of how many people they should expect to bring to Christ from the moment they arrive on the field."

I remember thinking, "Hmm... Try that in China, Russia, UAE, Egypt, or..."

In the early days of my missionary ministry, occasionally receiving questionnaires from churches that were supporting me caused me much personal angst. A church—usually looking for a reason to drop our support—asked, "How many people did you lead to Christ this past year?"

In South Africa, Zulu people readily agreed to bow their heads and ask Jesus into their hearts. Seeing any fruit indicating a true conversion was quite another thing, however.

My missionary friends in China speak of few conversions. In Europe, some missionaries report conversions are a rarity. Still, in the Middle East numbers and results—something American evangelicals thrive upon—are few and far between.

In my opinion, both the conference speaker and the pastor erred in their assessments. Interestingly, the director spent no more time living in another culture than did the pastor who spoke that morning. Besides a few missions trips out of the country, neither understood the intricacies of connecting with people in another culture.

The pastor in his intercultural naiveté oversimplified the issue. The conference speaker with his director's mentality uttered a narrow statement reflecting a CEO's perspective of navigating an organization. Neither view reflected an on-the-ground, long-term missionary perspective.

I suppose both were technically correct, but they were severely flawed, buried in their own exposures and viewpoints. Leadership that heads missions agencies often lacks one thing at the leadership level: missionaries themselves.

Goals Created in One's Own Image

Let me speak plainly here. The goals you initially set upon your arrival on the field—apart from learning the language and finding a place to live—will probably not see fruition. Not even close. Think about this for a moment.

What do you know about the culture of the people you're going to serve? How can you set accurate goals in a void of exposure and bonding with a culture in which you've never lived?

My initial understanding of the Zulu people and their culture filled my brain with all kinds of stuff. When I arrived in South Africa, Zulu people pointed out to me on many occasions that it's hard to fill a cup that's already full.[37] This meant: "You think you've got all the answers. What's left to talk about?"

Missionaries often construct their missionary goals from their own cultural setting and understanding of missions. This image dictates what missionary life and work should look like. Often these goals find formation outside the context of the very people and culture with which the missionary will live. The pieces don't fit. They *can't* fit. Square pegs never do fit into round holes.

This type of vision casting builds a ministry upon the missionary's cultural context rather than on the setting of the people among whom they will live. This is a sure way to ensure frustration and failure both for the missionary and nationals.

If you're an American, your goals are probably built around an ethnocentric, low-context, synchronic, guilt-cultured people. This is challenging if you're going to work in China. That perspective won't get you close to Chinese thought and life.

How much did I, a 28-year-old, Anglo-Minnesotan, passive-aggressive missionary in 1986, know about the Zulu people upon landing on the tarmac in Johannesburg?

Yes, I had studied their culture, but I was not of their culture. Yes, I had studied some Zulu before arriving, but I was barely able to converse. I had goals, plans, and aspirations, but most those ambitions were formed around my values rather than those of the Zulu people.

Know the Difference

If you're going to an African culture, it is likely that they view time sequentially. That's a big deal, believe me. It's better to leave your time schedules and deadlines back home. Time means something different in many other countries.

The Lewis model[38] describes three views of time in different cultures and people groups.

> **Multi-actives** are lively, loquacious people who do many things at once, planning their priorities not according to a time schedule, but according to the relative thrill or importance that each appointment brings. Italians, Latin Americans, and Arabs are members of this group.[39]

> **Linear-actives** plan, schedule, organize, pursue action chains, and do one thing at a time. Germans and Swiss are in this group.[40]

> **Reactives** prioritize courtesy and respect, listening quietly and calmly to their interlocutors and reacting carefully to the other side's proposals. Chinese, Japanese, and Finns are in this group.

Multi-actives talk most all the time. Linear-actives talk some of the time. Reactives listen most the of time, speaking little.[41]

Americans are linear-active. Time is linear, and we are often task-oriented, direct, frank, and punctually time-dominated.[42]

Zulu people are multi-active. They tend to be very relaxed about time, people-oriented, indirect, use lots of body language, and respect oratorical ability.[43]

This used to frustrate me to tears when I would arrive at one of our village churches. Regardless of the announced time, the Zulu people didn't begin readying themselves for church until they saw my vehicle peer over the hill. As my truck entered their village, only then did they begin readying themselves for church. It always required an hour's wait or more before services began. There's a reason for this: Zulus view time as sequential. And so the service began when everyone showed up, not at the time announced.

For me, as an American with a future-oriented, fast-paced, always moving forward view of time, church began when I arrived.[44]

Know the difference.

High-Context or Low-Context?

High-context cultures. Relationship building takes time and trust. An individual's identity is rooted in their family, culture, and work. Before getting to know a person deeply, one must understand their family background and members. Family is often everything. Often, understanding one's vocation points toward understanding the individual.

When communicating, Brian Neese of Southeastern University notes:

> Nonverbal elements such as voice tone, gestures, facial expression and eye movement are significant. Verbal messages are indirect, and communication is seen as an art form or way of engaging someone. Disagreement is personalized, and a person is sensitive to conflict expressed in someone else's nonverbal communication.[45]

Space is very communal in high-context cultures. In the United States while standing in a line at the post office, people usually stand at least three feet apart.

Standing in line at the post office in South Africa presented quite the challenge for me. There, Zulu people stand pocket-to-pocket. Your pelvis and buttocks literally touch the people in front and behind you.

These are just a few of the unique qualities of high-context cultures. Asian, African, Arab, Central European, Latin American, Mediterranean, and American-Indian cultures are generally considered to be high-context cultures.[46] "High-context cultures leave much of the message unspecified, to be understood through context, nonverbal cues, and between-the-lines interpretation of what is actually said."[47]

Low-context cultures. These have distinct contrasts. Brian Neese notes, "Cultures with western European roots, such as the United States and Australia, are generally considered to be low-context cultures."[48]

These cultures rely upon explicit communication, rather than the facial and body expressions and other nonverbal cues preferred in high-context societies.

Friendships form quickly and end quickly. Disagreement is not as personal as in high-context cultures. This is where many Western missionaries make egregious errors. Used to stating one's opinion—getting it off your chest—, Western missionaries are often unaware that when clearing their conscience with concise, stated opinions, they offend or dishonor a high-context person. Especially if these opinions are stated in front of other people. This brings public dishonor upon the person. It ends a relationship before it even starts.

For the low-context, learning takes place from specific to general. Neese again notes: "Learning occurs by following the explicit directions and explanations of others. Individual orientation is preferred, and speed is valued."[49]

Low context-cultures, such as English and Germanic speaking cultures, expect messages to be exact, explicit, direct, and detailed. This is quite a contrast to high-context cultures where metaphors, sagas, proverbs, and sayings appear ambiguous to the ears of low context-cultured people.

Knowing how to function among high-context and low-context people is the difference between effectiveness and failure.

Know the difference.

Guilt, Fear, or Shame?

Guilt-culture. America is a guilt-culture society. We value individual conscience. Guilt-culture societies concern themselves with an individual's level of guilt or innocence. Justice is key. People must follow the rules. Myriads of laws, ordinances, and orders ensure people do right. Follow the rules, or answer for your wrongs. One is guilty or innocent.

From the beginning of life, limitless rules and regulations keep people under control. To obey the rules makes one innocent. To violate the rules brings guilt and judgement.[50]

Personal standing in communities often hinges on one's adherence to the rules of a group. Good standing in communities requires obedience to the law. Demands for justice often voices itself as: "Who's to blame for this? Who will pay for this?" Fair play and justice is the highest marker of this group.

Shame-culture. Shame-cultured people value honor and loyalty above other considerations. Personal standing in a community depends almost entirely upon the honor others in that community perceive an individual to hold.[51]

In honor cultures, violence often becomes the tool to restore one's honor. A case in point is that of a Muslim father in Rocky River, Ohio, who shot his daughter for not respecting his rules about coming home on time and cleaning up her room.[52] Honor killings are all about restoring respect.

When a missionary encourages a shame-culture or high-honor person to receive Jesus as their personal savior, the question that person might think is, "How will this affect my family's honor?"

To respect one's ancestors is to honor one's family and name. This almost always takes precedence over all other considerations.

Fear-culture. In South Africa, —where we served— the Zulu people were very much a fear-culture people. In this culture the amount of power one used and possessed determined their standing. Such cultures are usually tribal or animistic.

Supernatural spirits or one's ancestors pressure people to conform by bringing harsh consequences upon those who dishonor their ancestors.

We experienced this regularly while ministering to Zulu people. The more rural the people, the more apprehension they had of allowing a white man into their circle of influence. Once I asked, "What causes you so much fear of me?" The Zulu woman replied: "Oh, I'm not afraid of you. Not at all. I am afraid that your presence will displease my ancestors—dead family members—, and they will punish me."

Curses and displeasures can be removed through incantations, spells, sacrifices, and spiritual world activities. Fear is what controls people and forces them to conform to the culture around them.[53]

Is the culture you're going to or currently serving a guilt, shame, or fear culture?

Know the difference.

Collectivism vs. Individualism

Daphna Oyserman, Heather M. Coon, and Markus Kemmelmeier from the University of Michigan present this psychology of cultural uniqueness:

> If you're American, you're from one of the highest Individualist cultures in the world. Individualism is not only desired, it's quintessentially an American thing. Hyper individualism marks our time.[54]

South Koreans are the exact opposite, forming one the most collective cultures. Here, honor, respect, and the group supersede individual considerations.

Individualism emphasizes independence, or control of one's self. One sets goals and accomplishes them to move forward. Fierce competition occurs for jobs, positions, and opinions. Uniqueness—individuality—is highly valued. Communication is direct and to the point.[55]

By contrast, collectivism emphasizes a sense of belonging over individual identity. Relationship with a group far outweighs individual considerations. Duty is more to the group than to oneself. Advice and consensus is sought rather than individual opinion.

In collective cultures, one alters oneself, according to the nature and makeup the group. Hierarchy outranks individual identity. These cultures prefer working in and according to groups.[56,57]

As a young man in South Africa, I learned to not look an elder Zulu man directly in his eyes. This was disrespectful. When making a decision that affected our ministry, all leadership needed opportunities to give viewpoints, advise, and process. We moved forward together, or we didn't move at all. Sometimes moving forward took months, if not years.

The older and more rural the Zulu team, the more collectively we functioned. The younger and more urban the members, the more individualistically our team worked.

Do You Know the Difference?

Is the culture where you will or currently serve sequential or synchronic? Some cultures spend time like money. You can save time, waste time, or spend time wisely. This is a great way of thinking about time if you're in North America, Germany, Sweden, or Holland.

It won't do you much good if you're living in South America, Southern Europe, China, or other parts of Asia. Why? Because those cultures view time synchronically. Time resembles a circle; it's not linear. Everything comes back around. Valuable relationships are those that go back and forth in time.[58] In the West, time moves forward, never backward. Know the difference?

Is where you're going to build your ministry a culture of an affective or of a neutral people? People in neutral cultures do not telegraph their feelings and emotions. They keep their thoughts and feelings subdued. Body language is almost nonexistent.

Affective cultured people show their feelings readily by smiling, frowning, laughing, yelling, leaving a group, or crying. This is may be OK in the United States, Italy, France, and Singapore.[59]

Americans "tell it like it is." This type of culture rubs many Japanese, British, Indonesians, Norwegians, and Dutch people the wrong way. Your first steps forward as a missionary in a new culture may become huge steps backward for a long time.

There is no one-size-fits-all with individualism and collectivism. Korean collectivism is different from Japanese collectivism. French individualism is different from American individualism. Not all experts agree on the definitions. All individuals within a culture are not imprisoned by the general characteristics of their cultures.[60]

Do you know the difference?

> "I try to find common ground with everyone, doing everything I can to save some. I do everything to spread the Good News and share in its blessings."
>
> The Apostle Paul, 1 Corinthians 9:22-23

Considerations

1. How can you gain deep, rich knowledge about the people you serve?

2. Describe the cultural differences between you and the people you are called to serve.

3. What changes in attitude and approach must you make?

4. What changes in your methodology are needed?

5. How do the national people you live among view you?

(16)

Missionary Success: What Is It?

"Success is not final; failure is not fatal: It is the courage to continue that counts."

Winston S. Churchill

A group of veteran missionaries—those who have served twenty years or longer— were asked, "What is the number one mistake missionaries make that leads them to resign?"

An elder missionary approached the microphone and said: "Comparison. Comparing their ministry to someone else's they consider more successful. That discourages most missionaries, I believe."

The Dangers of Comparison

When pastoring in Minnesota, I often traveled down to conferences held in the Twin Cities. Huge megachurches exist in the greater Minneapolis-St. Paul area. There are some great churches, led by brilliant leaders with a heart for God and people. Most of these conferences took place within their enormous church edifices.

Success for those churches revolved around—in part—big budgets, buildings, and crowds. Thousands of people. Large staffs. Millions of dollars. Professional musicians. Elaborate audio-visual systems. I have no criticism here. None at all.

I remember asking myself: "Don, what exactly is my win for my ministry? What does success look like for me?" Many pastors in smaller churches commented in our cluster group that those types of conferences did more to discourage them than to help.

For me, living in a town of 12,000 people put running a church of 20,000 per Sunday out of the question. While I enjoyed leading a staff of five, managing a staff of dozens like the big churches pointed to my reality. I had to find the win with my church staff not someone else's.

Spending time with staff and leadership, we hammered out what a win would look like for our congregation and community. Having an influence upon our area was attainable.

Much church success and goal-setting literature has one commonality: their definition of "success." Success is often about individual leaders reaching their dreams. Becoming personal successes. High numbers. Big budgets. Larger buildings. Lots of published books. Speaking engagements. Hey, no criticism here. God definitely calls people to such levels of engagement. But does that define success?

As a missionary, I always used to hesitate to give a report before a large group when I was following a report from a missionary from Kenya.

Once a wonderful missionary shared their work in Kenya. After starting dozens of churches, seeing thousands receiving Christ and hundreds baptized, a new Bible college started, three new clinics opened and . . . get the point?

Then it was time for me to give a report. Almost in shame, I reported of two new churches my first term and of barely getting a handle on the language.

Once after sharing in such a manner, a wonderful missionary couple followed me. This couple presented their report of serving in a most inhospitable place. In fact, not one person put their faith in Christ during their first term. Yet they beamed at God's calling in their lives. Their zeal and enthusiasm outpaced every other report given that week. They stated, "We know we are where God has called us."

Look at successful people in business, the pastorate, or on the mission field. Isn't success often judged by size and quantity?

Goal setting often consists mostly of individuals reaching the top of their professions, gaining notoriety, respect, wealth and power. Missionary do these sound like the goals of Jesus?

> "Whoever wants to be first must take last place
> and be the servant of everyone else" (Mark 9:35).

Hyper-individualism, which is so prevalent in the West, particularly in the United States, is a nonstarter in most cultures around the world. Often our idea of success focuses upon vision, drive, and the capacity to raise money and manage people. But that is going to wreck you out on the field. God does not call us to this type of success. He calls us to servanthood. One servant serves few at a small table and another servant serves many at a large table. It makes no

> God did not call you to success. He called you to servanthood.

difference. Both servants' faithfulness indicates success, regardless of the actual number sitting at the table.

Did we build a big ministry in South Africa over our twenty-two years? You bet. It's so effective that over seventy-five South African staff members are employed to ensure its success of serving the community. But we had a lot of little failures, too.

I can't take credit for all the current successes. South African leaders who came after me launched the current ministry into deep, glorious waters of faith. And God is really the one who deserves all the credit. Right?

You know what I consider our greatest success? Very few of those currently serving in our wonderful center know the name "Mingo." They do, however, know the name "Jesus." Every one of them.

Missionary, you've heard this before. It bears repeating. It's not about me or you. It's about *him*.

Relationship Is Goal-Setting

When I first arrived in South Africa in 1984, my heart was set on establishing as many churches as possible. I had a number firmly in my head. The problem with my thinking was that I focused on establishing churches before establishing relationships. Before establishing people.

My right-hand Zulu pastor, Simon Dube, sat down with me one day to speak of this deficit with me.

"Pastor Mingo," he said, "We Zulus are like your goats. You want us to go here and there, but you only care about the size of the herd, not the health of the goats."

Ouch. Simon's earthly Zulu wisdom spoken in broken English hit its mark.

As the churches grew, they began to falter. Growing people in Christ first marked a huge shift for us. Changing the soil we rooted people in—Christ, not my goals—produced stronger, more vibrant Christians. Simon's lessons always continued to challenge me in a better direction.

Once we planned a big day in one of our churches in the Zulu rural area of Matiwane, South Africa. Many Christians planned to travel long distances to attend that special Sunday.

As was my nature, I arrived that Sunday two hours before starting time. Upon my arrival, not a creature was stirring, not even a mouse.[61]

The church was locked; nothing was prepared for the big day. As the starting time slowly approached, my personal frustration level grew. Simon arrived fifteen minutes before services started. He saw my frustration and pulled me aside. I can still hear his words thirty years later.

> Mfundisi Mingo, there are two ways we can do this. One way is that I can try to assemble all twelve million of my Zulu people together. Once gathered, you can tell us Zulus how you want this day to go. Or maybe one Pastor Mingo can try to come our way—the Zulu's—a bit.

> Relax. We are Zulus living in rural areas. Many awoke early to travel far distances to be here today.

> Enjoy these people arriving this very moment more than you want your plans for the day. Your time is not that important. God and his people are.

Ouch again! Well deserved. Simon's lesson made a dent. This missionary was more concerned about punctuality, program, performance, and personnel rather than the actual people arriving that day. Focusing more upon connection rather than goal setting encouraged deep-rooted relationships and growth.

> Focusing more upon connection rather than goal setting encourages deep-rooted relationships and growth.

When I look back over my years in South Africa, it was relationships established that lasted. Relationships become the glue of ministry.

Understand First, then be Understood

Take an intercultural/cross-cultural Studies class. Study sociology and anthropology. Learn why people act the way they do. A bit of comprehension helps understanding of people's manners and considerations. Sit under a missionary who learned about a people rather than pushed the people to learn about the missionary.

Billy Graham valued his education in anthropology. It helped him understand people. Anthropology studies the diversity of human culture and language. Sociology concentrates upon complex social problems. These are two very good fields of study for missionaries.

Once during a meeting with our Zulu leaders, I showed public irritation with one of the members. As he droned on about a minor issue, my facial reaction showed frustration.

The next day, another of our older Zulu pastors visited my home. He explained that my expression of "anger" brought shame to the group the evening before. The accusation surprised me as I thought, "You've never seen me angry." Yet he made his point. I apologized to our leaders the next time we met and asked them to pray God would help me become a better leader. The apology did more to deepen our relationship than any Bible study I ever led.

Become Chameleons, not Crocodiles

To me, establishing good relationships between a missionary and local people resembles a chameleon approach.

Many a missionary—including myself—arrived at their country of calling brandishing big plans for ministry. They began aggressively moving citizens around like pieces on a chess board to suit a misunderstood image of ministry. This is a crocodile approach.

In Africa, we once watched a crocodile violently grab hold of its prey. Once securing its victim, the reptile begins twisting and turning to prey in the water to its liking. Missionary work, unfortunately, sometimes resembles this approach: twisting and turning people to conform to a missionary organization's plans and policies.

The chameleon, however, is a creature that blends into its environment. Good missionary cross-cultural effectiveness desires the foreigner—the missionary—to learn and become part of a culture before trying to command the people of that culture. Remember: When you arrive on your field of calling, you're the foreigner. You're the untrusted stranger. As a stereotyped American, you've got much to overcome.

I'm convinced missionary work is most effective when missionaries minister in the shadows of cultural existence, encouraging national people to lead their own people; not the other way around. Too often the missionary is viewed as "the boss."

Living among the Zulu people, I realized that on my best day my ability in the Zulu language was not nearly as proficient as one of our Zulu pastors on his worse day. I spoke the Zulu language, but Zulu people *are* the Zulu language. I understood the Zulus; they *are* Zulu.

Remember Your Mission

Christ clearly stated the ultimate mission of his Church. Some of his last words spoken before ascending into heaven were:

> Jesus came and told his disciples, "I have been given all authority in heaven and on earth. Therefore, go and make disciples of all the nations, baptizing them in the name of the Father and the Son and the Holy Spirit. Teach these new disciples to obey all the commands I have given you. And be sure of this: I am with you always, even to the end of the age." (Matthew 28:18-20)

A good diagnostic question to regularly ask in your missionary ministry is, **"How is what we are doing making Jesus followers?"** There are many good things that missionaries busy themselves with. How do those things bring people closer to Jesus Christ?

Considerations

1. What are your goals?

2. What does success look like to you?

3. How can you serve the people God has called you to serve?

4. How much do you know about the people God is calling you to serve?

(17)

Missionary Conflict

It's Not That Simple

One of the main tasks of theology is to find words that do not divide but unite, that do not create conflict but unity, that do not hurt but heal.

Henri Nouwen

Missionary conflict is often cited as the number one reason missionaries leave the field. Dozens of respectable missions agencies and sources appear to support this conclusion. They declare:

> The most common reason missionaries go home isn't due to lack of money, illness, terrorism, homesickness, or even a lack of fruit or response to the gospel. Regretfully, the number one reason is conflict with other missionaries. Yes, you read that correctly.[62]

You've heard it many times, that the number one problem with missionaries coming off the field and returning home is conflict. But I hold that it's not that simple.[63]

Most of the studies out there come from the eyes of the agencies, not the missionaries. This is not a criticism of the agencies. Agencies present their own perception.

This perspective is often an American denomination or church perspective rather than the individual missionary on the frontlines of service perspective. Pastors ask, "How do we keep our missionaries on the field?" This question—although very valid—lacks a missionary perspective. My question comes from a missionary perceptive: What are the real causes of missionary conflict in the first place?

Missionary service requires function in at least three complex worlds: their place of birth, place of missionary service, and their place with other missionaries. My purpose here is not to offer criticism, condemnation, or a preachy approach about such things. I merely offer thoughts to consider when dealing with the unavoidable; conflict. Mark it down. Whether you're close to Jesus in your walk or somewhere else, conflict always occurs. It's an inevitability of life.

> What are the real causes of missionary conflicts in the first place?

How Well Do You Know That Team?

In the business world, companies spend tons of money ascertaining the effectiveness of their teams. This involves understanding personality traits, temperaments, abilities, and skills of every team member.

DiSC® is a leading personal assessment tool used by over one million people every year to improve work productivity, teamwork, and communication.[64] Myers-Briggs is another popular personality assessment used when putting people together on a team. StrengthFinders is another valuable tool helping individual team members realize their strengths.

What is regularly practiced in the business world seems rarely considered when missionaries choose the teams—or are assigned to the teams—with whom they will work overseas.

Let's use the DiSC® method as an example. DiSC® is much easier to use and understand than other methods. And it works.

One important point: The main misuse of DISC or any other personality model is to assume that a person only has *one* trait. That is not at all the case. Each person has many traits to varying degrees.[65]

In the box I've created on the next page, you will notice four basic personality types: Dominance, Influence, Steadiness, and Conscientiousness. Study them closely for just a few minutes. The arrows show that no personality is all one type or another but rather a mixture of several types.

For example, some people are D & I personality types, while others may possess an I & S personality type. Most personalities lean toward one type more heavily than another.

Notice the chart on the next page.

Dominant
- Firm
- Direct
- Natural Leader
- Strong-willed
- Dynamic
- Often Extrovert
- Bold
- Must Be in Charge
- Needs Accomplishment
- **Task Keeper**

Influence
- Outgoing
- People Person
- Friendly
- Enthusiastic
- Promoter
- Lively
- Optimistic
- Positive
- Ignores Orders
- **Fun Keeper**

Task Oriented ↔ **People Oriented**

Compliance
- Analytical
- Precise
- Cautious
- Often Introvert
- Accurate
- Compliant
- Must Be Exact
- Thinking Oriented
- Needs Order
- **Order Keeper**

Steadfast
- Patient
- Loyal
- Even-Tempered
- Stable
- Workhorse
- Tactful
- Takes orders
- Harmony
- Work-oriented
- **Peace Keeper**

I've seen these four personality types demonstrated by an instructor with the simple function of needing a pen.

He walked over to an audience member, reached out, took the pen from her hand saying, "Hey, I just need to use this for a few minutes. Thanks." This is a High D personality approach.

The High I personality approach said, "Hey, happy people, I seem to be short of something to write with today. Which one of you beautiful people will let me use your pen? Thanks so very much. You're a big help."

The High S person fumbled around, diligently writing profusely with a stub of a pencil. Steadfast and loyal, the High S person plodded on, making an effort of it until someone offered them a pen.

The High C personality pulled out a brand-new box of twelve pens, aligning each one in exact order upon the desk and choosing one for that specific moment. A High C person is never caught without adequate writing utensils and implements.

Let's apply this to missionary teams.

Missionary Team One. The team consists of eight members: three married couples and two single missionaries. Four of the team members possess High D personalities. They are determined, strong, and confident. Three members are High S. And one member is a High C. What do you think this team will function like? Look back at the chart. See any problems here with four strong-willed, bold leader type personalities on the same team? What do you think?

Major Challenge is: _____

Major Advantage is: _____

Success Factor: Poor – 1 2 3 4 5 6 7 8 9 10 – Excellent

Missionary Team Two. This team is made up of six missionaries: three couples, and all their personalities are High S. They are loyal worker-ant type personalities. They're peace-keeping, humble people. This personality type is accustomed to following a laid-out plan and working to make it happen. What do you think?

Major Challenge is: _____

Major Advantage is: _____

Success Factor: Poor – 1 2 3 4 5 6 7 8 9 10 – Excellent

Missionary Team Three. This team is made up of two couples and one single missionary. Two members are very High I. Another member is very High C. The other two members are a mixture of S and C. What do you think?

Major Challenge is: _____

Major Advantage is: _____

Success Factor: Poor – 1 2 3 4 5 6 7 8 9 10 – Excellent

Missionary Team Four. This team carries a better balance. Of the four couples, one missionary lean towards a more D dominant personality. Two lean toward an I influence type personality. One is High C. The rest are S's.

Major Challenge is: _____

Major Advantage is: _____

Success Factor: Poor – 1 2 3 4 5 6 7 8 9 10 – Excellent

Famous High D Missionaries

Hudson Taylor, the father of faith missions, held a critical view of other missionaries in China in the nineteenth century. He was not happy with most missionaries he saw. He believed they were "worldly" and spent too much time with English businessmen and diplomats who needed their services as translators. Instead, Taylor wanted the Christian faith taken to the interior of China.[66]

When he started the China Inland Mission (CIM), Taylor was the dominant personality and pioneer behind launching the mission. He inspired literally hundreds during his life to enter China to serve as missionaries through CIM. God often places a strong leader to lead and cast vision.

David Livingstone—the great missionary and explorer to Southern Africa—held a very critical view of other missionaries in the region as well. He wrote: "The missionaries in the interior are, I am grieved to say, a sorry set . . . I shall be glad when I get away into the region beyond—away from their envy and backbiting." He went on to say, "That there was no more affection between them and himself than there was between his 'riding ox and his grandmother.'"[67]

Livingstone was a go-it-alone, High D type personality. It's interesting to note that the great missionaries often worked apart from other missionaries. This view takes nothing away from their accomplishments, but simply acknowledges the dominant personality type.

A High D person must be careful of arrogance, harshness, and bullying. They tend to push too hard, losing their team in the process.

A High I Missionary

Adoniram Judson, the great missionary to Burma, appears to have been a High I personality. Adoniram had an upbeat, inspiring personality. Judson looked for the opportunities of the day. He noted:

> A life once spent is irrevocable. It will remain to be contemplated through eternity. If it be marked with sins, the marks will be indelible. If it has been a useless life, it can never be improved. Such it will stand forever and ever. The same may be said of each day.[68]

Judson translated the Bible into Burmese, and his was the only translation available for decades. He planted the first seeds of the gospel in Burma.

He was full of energy, multi-talented, and very capable in multiple disciplines. Reading about his life, it appears he also struggled with the common weaknesses of a High I personality. Restlessness, search for purpose, and dealing with lack of results marked some of my findings in reading about his life.

Every team needs a High I personality. They energize people, encourage them, and bring fun to the party. A High I can find the best in people. A High I is usually everyone's friend.

They must be wary of their natural weaknesses, however. High I's need variety. They also can be disposed to boredom and struggle to follow through on tasks.

High S Missionaries

High S's are the backbone of every organization. They are the loyal worker ants. They get the job done. No organization can move forward without them.

High S missionaries make up the mainstay of the team. They are the unsung heroes of every successful organization. They served Hudson Taylor's team in China. These missionaries built the China Inland Missions and formed successful teams with Judson in Burma. They are the constant of every successful team.

One deficit is that they don't like change. They resist it mightily at times. They tend to do without purpose or goals. They need help making sure work is productive, not just busy.

High C Missionaries

No team functions effectively without a high C. High C's often are often a team's contrarians. Every team needs one. They ask questions like, "How?"

How can we do that? How can we find the money? How can we move forward? They can drive the rest of the team nuts.

In South Africa, I worked with a wonderful missionary. We became good friends. Rick is a High C personality. He likes order. He is cautious before embarking on a new venture. He thinks things through thoroughly and strategically.

By contrast, I am a High I with a handful of D sprinkled in. I drove Rick crazy sometimes with my bold actions, regularly stepping ahead of the team without consulting anyone. Patience, consideration, and respect won the day as we served well together.

High C's help keep order and structure. Their deficit is that they can become critical, demanding others be perfectionists. "If it's not done the right way, then I'm not doing it," becomes their mantra. High C's often baulk at faith endeavors. They think, "If I can't see it, how can it work?"

Conflict and the Team

How well do you know the team you're going to join? Can you work with them? It's tragically interesting that often a group of people—missionaries—gather together who could not work together effectively in any business setting. Their only commonality is that they bear the title "missionary." Simply being a missionary means that somehow all will miraculously gel together as a team. It rarely happens, if ever.

> How well do you know the team you're joining?

Isn't it interesting that a few years after Jesus's resurrection, the disciples individually went their own ways? Many built their own teams.

Paul and Barnabas had it out about John Mark. Paul confronted Peter publicly over his inconsistent treatment of gentiles. Paul was a High D. Peter was a High I. Barnabas was a High S. Dr. Luke, who authored the Gospel of Luke, appears to have been a High C personality. All these personalities staying together in a single, close group indefinitely was not strategic or possible.

What's Your Preferred Firing Order?

A key component of behavior in an individual is their firing order. The firing order consists of three elements: thinking, feeling, and action. The elements of the firing order can appear in any order.[69]

Feel—Act—Think. Some feel first, then act. Their empathy—or displeasure—for a person causes them to act toward the benefit of an individual, often to the detriment of the group or themselves.

Once during a business meeting in the church I pastored, a couple concerned with the salary of a staff member posed a substantial, immediate raise. The congregation agreed and voted to give the raise.

The problem was that the church didn't possess the funds at that time to actually fund the raise.

Although I pastored that church for less than a year, necessary changes were made to ensure a more orderly process on staff raises in the future.

Most people feel first, then act, and maybe—if at all—think afterward.

Act—Feel—Think. Others act intuitively. They go by their gut feelings. They possess a sense of their surroundings and act accordingly. Often their intuition leads them well apart from rationale for their reasons for making the decisions they do.

Their gut-feeling actions make it difficult for them to express the logic behind their decisions to others. Simply saying, "That's the way I feel about it," doesn't build confidence in a team.

Their act-first attitude sometimes causes regrets. Rather than act, they can react to a situation. They feel the consequences of their actions afterwards. And then thinking follows.

Think—Act—Feel. These types of individual tend to process an event by acting upon the available data. Their decisions are usually sound, but they are sometimes void of empathy.

There are other combinations, but the point is that people process events and act upon those events differently. Understanding each member's firing order is essential to understand and good communication.

What's your firing order? What's the firing order of your team members? Understanding each other's firing order helps missionaries know and work with each other.

Know Every Team Member's Personality Type

The better you know your team members' personalities, the healthier your interaction can be. Understanding their traits carries two major advantages. First, you harness their strengths. Second, you can make allowances for their deficits.

Rick, on a couple of occasions during our years together in South Africa, said: "Don, it's helping that I'm getting to understand your personality. You're an apostle Peter type personality." Rick was very gracious in seeking to understand and make room for me on the team.

Some Teams Will Never Work

Many missionary teams will never work. No matter how much you pray with each other. No matter how many mission statements you write. No matter how many team contracts members sign. Sincerity won't matter either. There is nothing this side of heaven that can make some teams successful and functioning. Their personality mix is too adverse.

Some team's traits are like nitrating glycerol and then attempting to mix it with white, fuming nitric acid. The result is an explosion. I've seen it too often. Mixing hyper-independents with team-oriented missionaries ensures problems. It doesn't matter if both sides love Jesus; it just won't work. It's better that each go their own way, forming or joining teams of better functionality. There is no shame in this. Joining a team that is doomed to dysfunction. is disheartening. And some missionaries do best as lone voices crying in the wilderness. Their personality style can never mix well with others. It's best to recognize this early.

The desired goal is to become a good fit and balance with other personalities. To join a group that you can work with, not struggle against. May missions agencies give more consideration to this crucial element of missions fluidity before sending missionaries out into service.

Understand Your Own Deficits

May I share gracefully—though in a not-so-tactful way—that perhaps your problem in getting along with your team, may be—ah, how can I say this—*you*?

Here's the thing. Every team I've served on or seen—regardless of its mission statement—was deeply flawed. It was faulty because each member on the team was a fallible being in a fallen world. "There are none righteous . . ." (Romans 3:10 KJV). Your entrance into a team brings another sin-injured person to that team. When conflict develops on a team, each missionary is a conduit of that conflict, bringing some level of dysfunction to their team.

> Each missionary is a conduit who brings conflict.

Check Your Own Soul First. Scripture is very clear on this point. How often do we as missionaries overlook or ignore this truth?

> Accept other believers who are weak in faith, and don't argue with them about what they think is right or wrong.
>
> For instance, one person believes it's all right to eat anything. But another believer with a sensitive conscience will eat only vegetables.
>
> Those who feel free to eat anything must not look down on those who don't. And those who don't eat certain foods must not condemn those who do, for God has accepted them.

Who are you to condemn someone else's servants? Their own master will judge whether they stand or fall. And with the Lord's help, they will stand and receive his approval. (Romans 14:1-4)

Considerations

1. What type of personality are you? High D, I, S, or C?

2. Describe the personalities of the missionary members with whom you currently or in the future will serve.

3. How will you make it work?

4. What is the greatest adjustment you will need to make to help your team's effectiveness?

(18)

Fruit Loops or Bran Flakes?

Missionaries remind me a lot of breakfast cereals. I love breakfast cereals. Like the old *Seinfeld* episodes where a dozen or more boxes of breakfast cereal lined Jerry's shelf above his kitchen sink. My eyes always peered to identify every single box on the ledge. I never quite made them all out. Missionaries are like that: so many different kinds, flavors, colors, and varieties.

Ever poured several breakfast cereals into a single bowl? You know, mix them all together? Fruit Loops, Sugar Smacks, Cheerios, and Wheaties into one big, beautiful bowl. It creates quite a mouth load of exploding sensations, let me tell you.

I've learned, however, that throwing a bunch of different cereals into a bowl simply because they share the commonality of being a breakfast cereal isn't always the best idea. Trust me on this one.

Many attempts made to discover just the right combination can produce some good results. Other cereal suicide-brews, however, proved too unpalatable to contemplate again.

Finding the right mix is the key. Blending wheat, oat, and rice flakes in harmony with just the right amount of a corn flour blend takes a skillful touch. And don't forget about the wheat flour, whole grain oat flour, oat fiber, soluble corn fiber, partially hydrogenated vegetable oil, salt, red 40, natural flavor, blue 2, turmeric color, yellow 6, annatto color, blue 1, and BHT for freshness.

Plus other considerations of sodium ascorbate and ascorbic acid, niacinamide, zinc oxide, reduced iron, wheat starch, vitamin A palmitate, color, folic Acid, vitamin D, and vitamin B12 added to the mix.

It takes quite a high dexterity to get just the right mix! Many challenges lay before a would-be successful cereal mixer.

Fruit Loops pushes its fruity flavor to tickle one's palate, all while Raisin Bran seems only interested in your colon.

While Cap'n Crunch captains his crunch, sometimes Sugar Smacks' sugary presence forces the Cap'n to walk the plank in your mouth.

Puffed Rice and Wheat? You can eat a whole bag and feel empty. Sort of like chewing on soggy air. I never understood the value of the puffed stuff.

My favorite breakfast cereal as a kid was Kaboom. To this day I regret the product being pulled from the shelves. Ah, how I miss the good old Kaboom days. Cereals were so much better back then.

Then, there's always sugary Frosted Flakes. *THEY'RE GREAT!* Braggard. Like Tony the Tiger is the only flake out there that matters.

Chucking a bunch of missionaries together reminds me of mixing all those cereals into one single bowl. Sometimes they mix well. Other times, well . . . it's sort of an ecclesiastical mess of sorts.

The biblical admonition for all the flakes, the Crunches, Loops, Smacks, Pops, Brand, Krispies, Puffs, Nuts, Charms—and even Tony the Tiger—is make your mix work. *Make it work*!

Is not the gospel about considering the other flakes in the bowl more than your own flake? That's in the Bible, you know.

Is there any encouragement from belonging to Christ? Any comfort from his love? Any fellowship together in the Spirit? Are your hearts tender and compassionate?

Then make me truly happy by agreeing wholeheartedly with each other, loving one another, and working together with one mind and purpose.

Don't be selfish; don't try to impress others. Be humble, thinking of others as better than yourselves.

Don't look out only for your own interests, but take an interest in others, too. (Philippians 2:1-4)

Act like a missionary for crying out loud. Years ago, I ignored a missionary and his guest from the United States while walking upon the boardwalk of Durban, South Africa. I saw him, ignored him, and walked the other way simply because we had had a disagreement.

I regret that to this day. Missionaries, if you've been in missionary service very long, here's the ugly truth: We missionaries can make quite a bowl of soggy fragments sometimes. Our flakes can diminish all the other flakes in the bowl. Don't become the soggy flake out.

Let's become the people we claim to represent. Jesus gave us our passports and identification papers. He said:

Your love for one another will prove to the world that you are my disciples. (John 13:35)

Did you catch that? It's not our education. It's not our philosophy of ministry. It's not the Boomer, Millennial, Generations X, Y, or Z leanings that show this angry, hateful world who we belong to. It's how we treat each other.

Wow. How we treat each other proves whether we are Jesus followers.

This is not a competition against each other, my missionary friend. It's a competition for souls against the Prince of this world. As we battle one another, at times it looks like we're losing more ground to the enemy slugging it out with each other on the front lines of missionary service. Every cross word, conflict, and action reflects upon those souls in the field you're trying to reach.

Once while attending a missionary's church in South America, a member asked me in broken English: "Does your group not have anything but children to send us? All they do is fight with each other." Sad, sad, sad. The Holy Spirit is grieved! Satan rejoices as conflict blocks people from Jesus.

> Let us purpose to be the people Christ redeemed us to become.

Let us purpose to be the people Christ redeemed us to become. The people Christ commands us to develop into as followers of him.

Let us be people of true love: God's love. That starts with each other. If you can't give deference, compassion, and forgiveness to that missionary you dislike, then perhaps a ticket home is a good choice.

You're just one beautiful flake in the bowl. Hey, you there. Yeah, you, Cap'n Crunch, called to serve on the island of Lake Wobegon. Give way to that dull, slow, bran flake missionary you think so little of. You need those kinds of flakes on your team. You can't fill the bowl by yourself.

Yes, hey you. Miss Lucky Charms. Your charm and whit worked well for you back home in your porcelain bowl. Here it's, ah, just a little different. These people in the jungles of Temperance River find you a strange oddity. A flake not to be trusted.

Don't get stuck on your own importance. Give way to those crusty old bran flakes in the missionary ranks. They've served a long time. They probably relate better to the people than do you. Remember, every team needs regularity to stay healthy.

What about you, sunshine? There's a time and place for Apple Jacks, but when things get tough out there in the Apostle Islands, you'll need those plain, unappreciated Cheerios on the team. They will steady your ship in stormy waters by their steadfast presence. Cheerios have stood the test of time. You're a newbie flake. Careful with your criticisms.

Corn Flakes, yes, you're a long-termer, too. I know you think your way is the only way, but give way to Cocoa Krispies. Those beautiful, dark chocolaty crisps bring much to the bowl!

Yes, that young, sugary, chocolate nugget seems cocky and arrogant, but you need their zeal and zing because sometimes your flake is a little dry.

I know. Where were these young upstarts in the beginning? When oatmeal was the only option? When oatmeal saved the day? Who needs all this new stuff? But you, oats, are not the only option now. Let the young, sugary flakes glimmer and shine! Be a bigger flake than that!

What makes the cereal aisle in the store such a delight to peruse? Variety. There's a time, place, and purpose for every box of their delightful entities on the shelves. This is what makes the breakfast corridor such an effective team and the best aisle in the store! Watch any little kid when they walk through heaven's gate into the world of sugary, happy boxes of artificial flavors, colors, and synthetically applied nutrients.

There's a big lesson to learn here: Let us become more than just a bunch of soggy flakes!

Consideration

1. What kind of flake are you?

2. How would you describe your interaction with other missionaries, team members, and support staff?

3. Look at Philippians 2:1-4. What is the one stand out quality you need to develop in your attitude?

4. What does your love for other team members look like?

(19)

Missionary Transitions

Causing Your Missionary Kid Pain

"You need to acknowledge that your choices brought pain to your child."[70]

Danica Newton, missionary kid and missionary

This chapter is written more for missionary parents, but it comes mostly from the perspective of missionary kids (MKs), and their perspectives about being Third Culture Kids (TCKs).

Wise missionary parents will read everything they can get their hands on concerning the development, psychology, and challenges of children growing up in a culture not belonging to their parents.

Please understand, missionary parent. Your decision to move your family to another country will open wonderful avenues of experience for your children. It will also cause them trauma and pain. Realizing this will go a long way to helping your missionary children deal with the challenges of becoming a Third Culture Kid.

> Your decision to move your family to another country will also cause them trauma and pain.

I've chosen to use the words "trauma" and "pain" because these two words come up often in conversations with Adult MKs. Spending almost all their developmental years in South Africa, my three adult sons humbly enlightened me to this reality.

As a missionary parent, my decision to move our three sons, ages five, four, and three years old at the time, to South Africa provided them with both rich experiences and pain. Let's frame this statement up a bit.

My oldest son, Donald, is now near forty years old. I asked him, "Son, how much pain did growing up as a MK cause you?"

He replied immediately: "I had a great childhood growing up in South Africa! I can't complain. I gained a broader sense of the world than many of my peers here in the United States. People who don't travel don't know what they don't know."

"But it's all those things I enjoyed growing up in South Africa that make me feel disconnected here in the United States as an adult. Many people's sense of who they are is developed by the geography they grew up in. Where I'm from isn't home any longer. My geographical location of origin is empty. I guess in that sense, yes it was and still is painful."

He shared other insights:

1. "Growing up in South Africa, I was always the American kid."

2. "Back in the States, I was always the South African kid."
3. "In South Africa, even though I sounded like my peers, I was never really one of them."
4. "Now living in America, I blend in well, but I'm not really an American. I don't think like Americans. The holidays don't have as much meaning. American values baffle me a bit."
5. "The two questions I'm asked that trouble me the most are:
    - 'Where are you from?'
    - 'Where is home?'"
6. "I have an internal sense that I don't belong anywhere."
7. "Extended family is distant. They're people you know about, but you really don't know."
8. "I wouldn't change where I grew up. It's just who I am."
9. "Yes, sometimes it's painful. Most times, it's wonderful."

Here's a truth. My decision to move to South Africa caused my three sons pain, plain and simple. You see, God called Kathy and me, not my sons, to serve among the Zulus. When I did this, my sons became Third Culture Kids or TCKs. That's not to say we made a mistake going to South Africa or that we regret the decision. It is to say that I wished we were more aware of the challenges they faced as missionary children.

> Our decision to move our three sons to South Africa caused them irrevocable pain.

I received an urgent message in my inbox on Facebook from a young missionary mother. Having just arrived for the first time on their field, she was concerned that her seven- and five-year-old children had started wetting the bed again. This missionary mom took her children to the doctor and found that nothing was wrong.

This was not the first time I had received such a call from a young missionary family. After about an hour of speaking with the parents, I assured them that most likely there was nothing to be overly concerned about. In fact, this happens a lot with young missionary kids. Their little worlds change so dramatically when they walk out of the airport holding onto their parents' hands, into a world they do not recognize or understand. They can't process that change rationally.

MKs Brains Struggle to Process Missionary Life

The brain has been described to me as consisting of two parts. In simple terms, one section of the brain is the rational part. The other is the emotional part. The emotional brain is almost fully developed by age eight, but the rational brain doesn't reach maturity until around age thirty. Guess which part of the brain a five-year-old missionary kid uses to processes a move to a different country, culture, and language? Children process missionary life through the lenses of an emotional rationale.

Recognize MK and TCK Trauma

MK children need their parents to recognize their trauma. Danica Newton, an MK and missionary, shares her intimate thoughts:

> When my parents came to me and acknowledged the trauma my siblings and I had experienced, when they apologized for the pain they had caused, they did not negate the Good Work they have done. They did not negate a lifetime of service for the Kingdom of God. They did not negate the fruit they had harvested for the King. Instead, they further confirmed Christ to us. The humble Man of Sorrows. The One who laid down His life. The One who sought out the voiceless, the weak, and lifted them up.
>
> Even though your choices to answer the Call of Christ caused trauma for your children—believe me when I say that they

have—your choices to give space for their pain can make way of healing. I ask you, on behalf of my fellow MKs both grown and still growing, to give this gift to your child.[71]

Help MKs Understand Their Full Identity

Our youngest son, Dennis, shared: "Finding who I was and wanted to be was a challenge. It's still challenging. While there's a lot of things I appreciated about my upbringing, this is one of my greatest challenges."

Another of our sons, Daniel, shares:

> A huge issue for an MK is their identity. If you don't teach a child that their identity is in Christ, then it is very easy to identify yourself as only an MK. What happens if that is stripped away? What happens when you leave the nest or the field?
>
> When my parents left missionary life to pastor in Minnesota, that was something I had to figure out. I was no longer an MK. Who was I? Well, I was Dan, God's masterpiece created for a purpose.
>
> I think too many MKs get caught in the identity of the "MK" They try to live up to a concept rather than what God wants for them. If you can't grasp God's will for you, and you are trying to live out God's will through your parents, it will derail you. You will always feel like you failed.
>
> The missionary needs to teach their child that they are made in God's image to be something incredibly unique for his glory. That means something separate from what their parents are doing. At some point you are no longer an MK.
>
> I am still a Mingo, and my parents are again missionaries, but I am not. I am, however, a man that was raised on the mission field

and saw incredible things done for God through my family that shaped me to form my own identity and own calling.

Understanding Your MK's Quirks

During our first term in South Africa, which lasted almost six years, we returned to the United States for a much-needed furlough. When we entered a grocery store in Dallas, Texas, our sons went nuts when we arrived at the breakfast cereal aisle.

In South Africa in the late 1980s, worldwide sanctions imposed against the government meant few, if any products from the United States were available in South African grocery stores. Everything needed was obtainable, but little variety existed. We ate Weet-Bix, ProNutro, Jungle Oats, and a host of other South African products. Cereal aisles at the time were limited.

As we turned the corner into lane 7 in an American grocery store on our first day back, a cornucopia of brightly colored boxes displayed a vast array of cereal choices. Our youngest son, Dennis, yelled, "Hey, guys, look at this!" As our sons ran up and down the gauntlet of Cocoa Puffs, Sugar Smacks, and other sugar-laden items packaged to catch a child's eye, a shopper nearby queried, "What's wrong with those children?" Turning, I replied, "Nothing, it's just the first time they've ever seen this much cereal before. You see, we are monks living in a monastery. We don't get out much." The blank stare on her face at my comment communicated my message, "Please mind your own business."

Recently, Kathy and I visited a church during Sunday morning service. We watched a young missionary family just returning from a third world country for a furlough.

Behind me a voice whispered, "What's wrong with those children? They are so loud and noisy." I turned and smiled, replying gently, "They've just returned from living for four years in Africa. They're adjusting. They are perhaps nervous as this is all foreign to them."

> They were born here, but home is over there.

The lady replied, "But, they were born here. Weren't they?"

Smiling, I replied, "Yes, but home is over there."

Voices from MKs

I asked several groups of MKs and TCKs, "What was the hardest part about being a MK?" I received many replies back from MKs as young as ten years old and others in their fifties. Here are their responses.

Dennis, my son, shares:

Everyone wanted to know the missionary kid, but no one wanted to become your friend because you wouldn't be around long enough.

People treated us like superheroes, but not friends. When I was in college, there wasn't one group of students I could identify with. That is still a challenge today.

To this day, I struggle to know where home is or should be. Home is often where your friends live.

Rachael:

As an MK, I wish my parents had taken us to see where we were going to serve before we moved there. I realize this would have been hard and expensive with five kids, but I think it would have helped with adjusting to life on the field a bit faster.

Kathy:

One of the hardest parts of being an MK was that nothing I did was ever enough. We always had to be better. When we were in the States looking for support, we would always be asked to sing. We felt like performing monkeys on a stage—if we gave a good enough impression, we'd get the support—and if not, then we didn't get support. I do have to say that the good outweighed the bad. My dad was also an MK—so I saw my grandparents and my parents as missionaries and the many things that they all went through. And now I'm in the same boat.

Alicia, a missionary mom:

We are only three months in but have already jumped some hurdles with our ten and eight-year-old. Some tears have been shed over feeling forgotten by their friends back home. It was something I personally prepared for but didn't think about our girls feeling that way.

Also, I have seen it is hard to connect with people quickly when they don't feel like have anything in common. We've had to give them some verbal cues in the social skills category.

Another Rachel:

Friends moving around. Not having stable friendships. I felt rootless and far more interesting than fitting in.

Ana:

I feel like for me it is the feeling of belonging. As a missionary kid you are a third culture kid, so you are used to combined cultures.

Consequently, it makes it harder for one to settle and have a feeling of belonging to just one culture.

Joshua:

It's hard for me to say, "This is the hardest thing." There are so many things fighting for that #1 spot, but I'll go with this: I find it hard to maintain my friendships with people having said so many goodbyes and having so many long-distance friendships. After so much grief over goodbyes, I find myself shying away from making new friends.

Derek:

Being told where home is.

Jordan:

Not truly fitting in anywhere.

Beth:

Always being a misfit.

Michelle:

Struggling with wanting to "belong" somewhere. I am the fourth generation in missions in my family and I see how much grief sometimes unacknowledged from loss from the many "goodbyes" that have affected our family.

Brianna:

It's hard for me that I look like I belong here, but don't feel like I belong here at all. I feel like I'm always misunderstood. It also gets tiring for me that I'm always running every interaction through two cultural frameworks. In Mexico, I didn't feel that way—life just felt right. Now life seems more complicated.

Scott:

The feeling of never being fully understood except by other MKs. No one really knows me fully because there is always one side of me that I'm not showing. I feel like I almost must deny part of me to just survive; especially here in the U.S.

Maria:

Yes, and yes and yes to all of the above. Like Joshua said . . . having to say so many goodbyes can cause someone to lose the desire to nurture friendships . . . and for me, if I may be honest here . . . this is an ongoing battle even today for me. The amount of effort of building, nurturing, and pouring myself into a friendship diminishes as I look at the possibility of saying goodbye.

At times I think, "What is the use of building relationships if we will say our goodbyes in the end?" Sounds selfish, but, honestly, that hinders me from making new friends.

Abigail:

For me the hardest part about being an MK is always feeling different from everybody else. I think the hardest part is being homeless.

Everywhere I go, for as long as I can remember, I'm the guest, the foreigner, the stranger. I can learn to blend in anywhere, but I don't belong anywhere. I'm almost eighteen and I've been on the mission field for fourteen years.

Bekah Lou:

I think the hardest part is finding where you belong and realizing that no matter how hard you try, you don't ever fully fit in. And losing a lot of relationships.

Lynette:

I lived in Ethiopia for three years when I was aged nine to twelve. Two things come to mind. When we returned to Minnesota I wanted and tried to share my experiences with other children, but no one cared or wanted to listen. I think some thought I was bragging. I wasn't, though. I was just excited to share my experiences. It made me feel like an outcast. Like I did not belong. Another thing was the American world continued while we were gone. Other children ridiculed me because I did not know about common things. It was very difficult to be so different and not know things that were common about America.

A Sixty-Year-Old Woman MK:

I think I'm still unraveling more and more of this. Right now, I'm trying to deal with stressed/strained family relationships that were under a lot of pressure because of being on the mission field. I've also been wrestling for a couple years now with the fact that some of the decisions my parents felt called to make were not what was best for me. I believe that God is sovereign and that he is good. I don't know how to reconcile that with some of the hurt I experienced as a direct result of my family's calling.

Deborah:

One HARD part of being a MK is all the goodbyes! We left loved ones in America. We knew we'd probably never see our grandparents again. With going to boarding school we had so many goodbyes with our parents. I suffered a lot of homesickness. I missed my parents from first through twelfth grades. After having children, I had to deal with abandonment issues from so much times away from parents! I didn't find stateside expectations for MKs that bad, but I think many did!

Mary:

I think it is hardest when you are a combination of cultures. Sometimes you react to situations in a way that is culturally unacceptable where you are, and sometimes that is because you are putting forth a combination of all of them. You end up with your own unique culture which nobody understands, except other third culture kids. When it comes to us, we can understand and respect the culture confusion in each other even when those cultures are different. I am thirty years old and spent fourteen years on the field with my parents.

Martha:

Finding who YOU are! Growing up you're always the missionary kid, whether it's in your home country or on the field. Some of us don't really get to discover who we truly are as an individual until many years later. Some of us still struggle with it.

Helping Your MK Celebrate Their TKCness

Growing up as an MK presents many advantages, too. Capturing these advantages depends largely on you—the missionary parent—catching special moments for your child. Here are some suggestions to ponder.

Pull Down Your Defensive Walls

MKs sharing their pain and trauma of missionary transitions with their parents requires a nonaggressive response by parents. One missionary parent said, "Oh, she's not going to lay that one on me."

Missionary parent, your MK's health begs for an honest exchange of thoughts and feelings. Encourage them to express their understanding and processing of their MK life. Don't be defensive about such conversations. Be unoffendable in such dialogues.

How Does Your Missionary Life Affect Your Children?

Many missionary parents share their ignorance of their children's struggles in this area. One adult MK shared some thoughts to combat this.

A missionary parent needs to regularly ask their MK's:
- What is your greatest struggle right now about being a missionary kid?
- What do you like most about being a missionary kid?
- What do you like least?

> "Least" is a preferred word over "hate." Instead of saying, "I hate this or that about being a missionary kid," encourage them to say, "This is what I like least about it."

- Ask, "How can we make this better for you?"

What's Going on in Your MK's Soul?

Understanding the health of your MK's soul is a high priority. I often thought, "What does it matter if I build a big ministry, if I lose the soul of my children in the process?" My first responsibility was to them, before ministry.

Supporting churches often asked Kathy, "What do you do on the field?" She always responded, "My first responsibility is to my family. My sons are my first church. They are my disciples I try to raise to love Jesus."

Make a BIG Deal Out of Little Things

One Christmas Eve in South Africa, I stood in line—or the queue, as it's called—in the post office. It was a typical December day. Blazing sun, high temps, and people standing shoulder to shoulder sweating profusely all over each other in a smelly Ladysmith post office.

When I presented a parcel slip to the clerk, she gave me a huge box. Entering our house with the box, our three sons crowded around it as we opened it.

Inside the box were unexpected Christmas gifts from a supporting church in West Kansas. Each gift carried a name on it. As we placed the wrapped gifts under our Christmas tree, one of my sons asked, "Why did they send us Christmas presents, Dad?" I replied, "Because you're missionary kids! You're special. This church appreciates each one of you." Thirty years later I can still see the smiles that produced on their faces.

Wake Up and Smell the MK's Coffee

An adult MK shared, "We spent our entire lives in a car, at an airport, or on a plane traveling here and there. I just wished we could have stopped sometimes to look around."

Missionary parents tend to wrap themselves up in their calling and ministry. Dad, Mom, please remember this: You chose your missionary life. Your children did not. MKs need to live a kid's life, not a missionary's life. Their needs are wrapped up into their emotional little brains and souls. They don't process the call of God. Reaching the world for Christ is a tough one for the average parishioner to grab hold of let alone your eight-year-old MK.

Suffer not your little MK children to come unto you, forbid them not, for such is the kingdom of heaven.

Think about it.

Parents, let your MKs help plan your trips. Ask them for input. My sons still talk about seeing the Colosseum in Rome. Flying back and forth from South Africa usually required a layover somewhere. So when laying over in London, for example, we experienced London.

Dad, stop the car—for more than just bathroom breaks! I confess my own fault here. In the early days of deputation and fundraising, this task-oriented father drove from point A to point B in the shortest amount of time. Hours spent on the road were simply an exercise in getting from one place to another. I quickly learned to take time for fishing, sightseeing, and other possibilities that interested my sons.

Dad, stop the car. Get out. See the mountains. Go on a hike. Catch some fish. Take some pictures. Go to Six Flags and Disney World. Don't be too busy. Your MKs will love you for it.

Dad, are you listening?

Pay your kids to help. During our furloughs when our sons accompanied us, it was their responsibility to set up our display, give out prayer cards, and talk to others about South Africa. Often people remarked, "How do you get your sons so involved?" My answer usually produced a laugh of disbelief. I said, "I pay them." And pay them we did.

A certain percentage of every love offering or honorarium was split between our sons. This helped them feel part of our ministry. You perhaps react, "Why would I pay my kids?" My answer, "Ah, *you* get paid. Don't you?"

Encourage Your MK to Develop a Hobby

A missionary friend of mine tells of his son's love for amateur ham radio. His son spends hours a week talking to other ham radio operators all over the world.

A missionary daughter I know makes porcelain dolls.

Another MK collects stamps. He plans to pay for his entire college education by selling his stamp collection. He has collected pages of stamps at every stop while traveling as a MK. Here's a cool aspect to this story.

Informed of his parents' destinations, he regularly asks them to stop at certain destinations so he might purchase pages of stamps at local post offices. It requires a great deal of planning on all their parts. He loves MK living because of his stamp-collecting excursions.

Another teenage MK talks incessantly about coffee. This MK, who is an expert coffee snob, samples coffee at local destinations all over the world. He's forgotten more about coffee than I'll ever understand.

He talks about coffee bean oil content, types of bean roasts, coffee drippers or aeropresses, blends, single origins, varietals, processing, soils, altitudes, taste, acidity, smoothness, and other facets I don't pretend to comprehend.

Missionary life for him is about experiencing new coffees, from the fields they're harvested to the café's they prepared.

Missionary parents, make time for your MK's hobby. Set its importance to be almost equivalent to your ministry. Because, after all, your family is your ministry. Right?

Family Meal Times: A Most Important Asset

Some of our best family experiences occurred during the evening meal around the dinner table. We talked and argued about a host of issues. We still reminisce on those great times around our table.

Learn to revel over every good thing that happens in your missionary family. May your MKs look back on their TCK childhoods with fond memories.

Considerations

1. How can you help your children with missionary transitions?

2. What can you do to help your MKs make long-lasting friendships?

3. When do you discuss TCK challenges with your children?

4. Where can you discuss this? Examples: Zoo? Park? Dinner table?

(20)

When Your MKs Leave Home

I'm not going to sugar coat this with spiritualizing words and platitudes of, "Just trust God." Here's the gut-wrenching truth: When your children begin leaving and heading for life back in your country of birth, it's a killer. For me it resembled more of a funeral than a celebration.

It's funny that a lot of the folk encouraging me to "trust God" as my sons began leaving for college eight thousand miles away suffered the agony of sending their little girl to university only two hours away from their home.

The empty-nest stage of life sees the second highest percentage of missionary resignations. I still remember vividly to this day almost twenty years ago, when I accompanied my oldest son to Florida to help him get settled in college. Our two younger sons were still in high school in South Africa, necessitating that Kathy stay back.

> The empty-nest stage sees the second highest percentage of missionary resignations.

The morning I left the hotel in Pensacola, Florida, to catch my plane back to South Africa, I drove past the dormitory. I looked up to the third floor at the room where my oldest son, Donnie, was staying. The light was on in his bathroom. My soul wept.

Reshape Your View

So many missionary parents view this time as a time of loss. Understand that your MKs leaving the nest is not a loss, but rather a necessary, healthy transition.

Yes, the moment is particularly tough for missionary parents. Kathy and I were in South Africa while all three of our sons were in Florida at college.

We acknowledged our emotions about the transition. It was difficult. We didn't need to apologize to anyone for how we felt. At the same time, sharing our pain with American friends was an experience of apathy rather than empathy. One friend said, "Everyone's kid has to leave home." I thought this was an interesting comment considering that their twenty-eight-year-old son still lived at home at the time.

We learned to understand that our sons leaving home was a natural, necessary passage of life. To make the transition easier, we:

1. Flew all our sons back to South Africa for their next couple of Christmases.
2. Also brought them back their first two summer vacations.
3. Traveled more frequently to Florida to see them and help us deal with the transition.
4. Started saving money ten years earlier to provide for such trips.
5. Relied on email, which helped. There was no Facebook in those days.

Here's the thing. While you're weeping as they walk out the door, your young adult children burst through doors of opportunity with anticipation and adventure. Encourage their excitement rather than pouring a spirit of guilt over them for leaving you. How you view your MK's leaving the nest affects everyone's emotional health.

Don't Be a Debbie Downer

A while back, *Saturday Night Live* developed a character named Debbie Downer, who was played by Rachel Dratch. Debbie Dower ruined everyone's time on every occasion.

At Thanksgiving she talked about food poisoning. At Disney World, after being hugged by Pluto, she says, "Oh, hi, Pluto. It must really be fun working at Disney. Although at any major theme park, you live under the constant threat of terrorist attacks." She continues to talk about Disney World, saying, "I love Disney World. It reminds me of my childhood. I mean, before my two-year stint at Children's."[72]

Debbie Downer ruined every party and gathering. Everyone dreaded her appearance, and no one wanted to be around her. Don't be that Debbie Downer to your MKs. Be positive and upbeat. This can be an exciting time of life for your MKs, but not if you're incessantly whining about it. Missionary parent, your MKs will avoid your presence if you continually present such an attitude.

Your Relationship Is Changing, Not Ending

Missionary parents going through this stage of life often view it as a permanent separation. May I say gently from experience that you'll gain more than you'll lose. Yes, it's difficult, but life is full of such necessary, difficult, yet healthy transitions. How you handle your life transitions will determine your soul's health and the health of your family.

Explore Your New Life

Take up photography. I've become a decent photographer. Not professional, just decent. I shoot nature photos because I love nature photography. My oldest son is a professional photographer and gives good advice as we look through my photos.

Uploading hundreds of photos to my Facebook and Unsplash accounts brings pleasure. I love the solitude, creative process, and sharing my photos. Others often encourage me to enter photo contests. Pleasure comes from the pure enjoyment of seeking out meaningful shots.

Start a blog. I started a blog a few years ago. An editor of a monthly magazine read some of my blogs and encouraged me to write. This book is my fourth. Writing and journaling brings a sense of release and expression. And who knows where my writing can lead. Although, I write for the pleasure of writing, not with the expectation of making money.

You know the most popular book outside the Bible in the evangelical world today? *Jesus Calling* is the number-one selling book. Did you know the author's—Sarah Young's—books have sold more than ten million copies? And Sarah and her husband are missionaries.

Draw. Paint. Create. Take a class. One missionary I know is a certified Bob Ross instructor. I'm amazed at the artistic creativity of some people. Another missionary makes porcelain dolls. One missionary builds furniture. Find something you love to do outside your ministry.

Start a garden. I know several missionaries who enjoy gardening. Many plant vegetable gardens. The exercise is good. It focuses one's mind on a single task. And it provides cheaper, healthier food!

Cook! My brother is a wonderful cook. I enjoy listening to him talk about preparation of the meal. For him, it's a source of joy. He loves to entertain folk at the dinner table.

There are a number of missionaries out there who are killer cooks. A few minister through cafés on their fields of service.

Social media. Today we are fortunate to enjoy social media. We regularly see pictures and videos of our grandchildren. Our sons video-call regularly.

While relationships change, they grow closer in other ways. To video chat with our grandkids is a highlight. With Marco Polo, Instagram, and Facebook, staying in touch is easier than ever!

Become a coffee connoisseur! If you like coffee—and I do—, check out different types of coffee available in your area. Do you prefer a dark roast or light roast? Kenyan, Costa Rican, Haitian, or Turkish? A cappuccino, mocha, latte, flat white, espresso, ristretto, long black, café Americano, café macchiato, affogato, Vienna, black eye, café Cubano, iced coffee, iced mocha, or frappuccino?

These days I lean more toward a good Americano. You can't mess that up.

Did I say I love coffee?

Fall in love again! Start dating. Lay a big kiss on her. Go ahead! This time you won't hear voices saying, "Ick, that's gross!" Empty nesting is not all bad!

Find ways to romance and spend time together. Learn to think about each other again like you did when you first met. The practical side of this practice is that it helps keep you from continually thinking about and missing your adult children.

Take those travel opportunities. As missionaries, you often find yourself on layovers while traveling. Take a couple of extra days and make your layover a stayover. See the world. Do what many empty nesters wish they could do, but either are not healthy enough or do not possess the money to do.

Transitions on the 7s

A popular big city radio talk news show gives traffic reports on "the 7s." At 07, 17, 27, 37, 47, and 57 minutes into each hour, a traffic report comes to their listeners. For Kathy and me, it seems like most of our major transitions of missionary life were also on the 7s.

By our seventh year of marriage, all our sons were born and heading into their adolescent years. It's during this time that we as young missionaries underwent great challenges of missionary life. We finished schooling, continued training, completed internships, received the approval of our missions agency, and raised our support. Our seventh year of marriage landed us in South Africa for the first time. Consider all those transitions in just the first seven years—they were monumental!

By year fourteen of our marriage, our children had entered into their teenage years. With several years of missionary service under our belt, our teens added a unique element to missionary living. Navigating the waters of raising teenagers on the field and dealing with the complexities of overseas life creates different nuances. These were challenging distinctions unique to missionary life.

In year twenty-one, our children begin leaving their nest, heading off to make their own way in life. We were missionary parents entering our forties and heading into our fifties.

By year twenty-eight, most of our children were gone. We traveled back and forth for graduations, weddings, and so many other life events that it was hard to keep track of the time zones, let alone life. Jet lag became a not-so-strange stranger.

Then a new, gloriously difficult transition of missionary life began to take place: GRANDCHILDREN! Those wonderful, beautiful grandkids who swell the heads of grandparents with so much pride they almost burst a blood vessel!

The grandchildren stage is probably the second most difficult time for older missionaries. Kathy and I currently have fifteen grandchildren, who live all over the United States.

A disconnect often takes place between missionary grandparents and their grandkidos. Their desire to travel back home for every major grandchild event soon reveals the reality of the impossible.

Year 35, your adult children are probably well settled now where they live and work. Your MK's that never really knew a place called "home" in their country of birth endeavor to forge a home where they live.

Adult MKs end up living all over the place, far away from their missionary parents. Our sons currently live in California, Georgia, and Florida.

As older missionaries, you will travel large distances to see your children and grandchildren. This comes with the calling. It's the cross a missionary must bear.

You're Still Loved and Needed

Yes, relationships change during all these transitions. Recognize that you are still loved and needed even though you perhaps feel like a lonely, forgotten person. While your adult children grow into new roles, you will need to do so as well. This is necessary for a healthy life.

> Your relationships can grow and become closer by positively accepting transitions.

Your relationships can grow and become closer, not more distant, with your adult MKs if you recognize and accept such changes.

Mayo Clinic in Rochester, Minnesota, has four important tips to help with the empty nesting stage of life:

Accept the timing. Avoid comparing your child's timetable to your own experience or expectations. Instead, focus on what you can do to help your child succeed when he or she does leave home.

Keep in touch. You can continue to be close to your children even when you live apart. Try to maintain regular contact through visits, phone calls, emails, texts, or video chats.

Seek support. If you're having a difficult time dealing with an empty nest, lean on loved ones and other close contacts for support. Share your feelings. If you feel depressed, consult your doctor or a mental health provider.

Stay positive. Thinking about the extra time and energy you might have to devote to your marriage or personal interests after your last child leaves home might help you adapt to this major life change.[73]

Considerations

1. What transitions are you currently experiencing?

2. What's your plan to deal with your transitions?

3. Who can you talk to? Who will you talk to? When?

4. What adjustments must you make?

5. How can you see God working in the midst of your transitions?

(21)

When Your Brook Dries Up

In the 17th chapter of the book of 1 Kings a missionary story unfolds. In the Old Testament, Elijah resembles a modern-day missionary (without all the killing of the prophets of Baal stuff).

Think about it: He traveled continuously. Shared God with many doubters. Spoke the words of God. Confronted unbelief. Encouraged reliance upon God. Lived and depended on donations from others. Faith marked his life. He was a traveling missionary.

Okay, okay, yes, he was a prophet. Calm your theological fears. My point is, his lifestyle—at least, to me—resembles a modern-day support-raising missionary who leaves his home and roams from place to place sharing the message of God with doubters and unbelievers, while helping widows and orphans along the way.

In 1 Kings 17, God called Elijah to a special place: the Kerith Ravine. There, God met his needs after announcing a severe drought was on the way for everyone else. God provided plenty of water for the parched missionary prophet while others suffered in a parched land.

God met Elijah's essentials in a most unique fashion. God supplied Elijah with exactly what he needed. What I like to call the Raven Rendezvous Restaurant provided meals on wheels delivery service to Elijah every day. Things were perfect. Until, after a long while in a demanding season of missionary service, Elijah's brook dried up.

Have you ever experienced a barren brook season of life and ministry?

When your largest contributor stops supporting you?

When no matter what you've tried, you just can't gain those last few supporters needed to supply your ministry?

When your sending church suffers a devastating collapse after the senior pastor's retirement? Perhaps contributions take a steep dive, and the church that was "going to be behind you no matter what" ceases to exist, and you lose twenty-five percent of your finances in the blink of an eye.

When your home church's interest in your ministry dries up. For whatever reason, they simply don't care as much for you or what you do.

When your missions agency changes policy, structure, and requirements, leaving you with huge decisions to make regarding your future with the organization.

When your denomination experiences mass defections of churches due to controversial issues among its pastors, which have little to do with the missionaries out on the field.

You begin to receive letters stating, "We don't support missionaries any longer from your denomination, fellowship or group." They aren't always nice when informing you. Then your ardent, count-on-us supporters drop you.

When your organization cuts their missionary workforce by fifteen percent, citing fund shortages.[74] Most the cuts affect the older, more experienced missionaries.

When the exchange rate in your country cuts your finances thirty percent in one month.

When violence and political unrest erupt, forcing you to cancel activities and leave your home to find a safer place for your family.

When the country in which you're serving imposes new taxes upon you that effectively decrease your disposable income by fifty percent.

When your health dries up.

When your adult MK goes off the rails into drug abuse, alcoholism, agnosticism, or something else that is tragic.

When some horrible thing happens to you.

What are you going to do then?

Missionary, what are you going to do when your brook dries up? Most missionaries experience at least one, if not many brook drying seasons of ministry and life. Elijah's exchange with God offers several health-steps. I prefer to call them steps to soul-health. Let's look at them.

> How you react to your brook-drying seasons of life determines the amount of time you spend in your cave.

You may need to adjust your ministry and location (1 Kings 17:9). It seems God often uses brook-drying scenarios to move us into new stages of opportunity. Sometimes that horrible season you're experiencing is the only means by which God can convince you to make a huge move in your ministry or location. Elijah moved and met the widow at Zarephath.

Why leave a brook and move in with a poor widow? Why leave where you are and move to that place? A dry brook may point you in a uniquely different direction.

We learn to look to God to supply our needs when our brook dries up. Before you write that letter, email, MailChimp, or some other form of communication asking for supplemental brook-drying income—give it to God first. Give God a shot!

Then get ready. The sources from which God supplies may surprise you! Watching God work and supply our last few years amazes me. I'm in awe of God and his people (1 Kings 17:7-10).

Here God used a poor desperate widow and her son. In blessing Elijah, God blessed her family, too. God's provision often comes from the humblest of sources.

God supplies even in the most meager of times. As the nation Israel struggled, Elijah and the widow's family enjoyed ample provision. Provision may seem less than desired, but God's provisions serve a greater purpose than just filling one's immediate need.

Do you really need everything you possessed when your brook flowed full and freely? What adjustments can you make to maximize the now barely trickling creek in your life? Perhaps it's time to get rid of some baggage.

Remember, give thanks for both the fast-flowing rivers and the slow, trickling creeks in your life. God is provider of them both.

More trials, struggles, challenges, and tests follow. Sometime later, the widow's son became extremely ill. The widow railed on Elijah in her moment of desperation. Desperate people sometimes attack those they view as religious or closer to God. As one young Zulu mother demanded of me, "Why did God do this? Why did he let my baby die? What do you say to this?"

The widow's comment to Elijah is most interesting. She cries, "What do you have against me, man of God? Did you come to remind me of **my sin** and **kill my son**?" Apparently, something from her past haunted her. She believed her hardships were punishments from God.

When was the last time you thought, "What must I have done wrong for God to allow my ministry to go like this or that?" I've thought this before. I've heard other missionaries say this, too. Here's a possible answer: nothing!

Perhaps your dry brook is an opportunity for faith. Testing builds maturity (James 1:2-4). God is big about maturing us in our faith towards him.

After Elijah prays for the widow's son to be healed, God raises the boy from the dead.

Notice the change in the widow's attitude. She announces, "Now I know that you are a man of God and that the word of the Lord from your mouth is the truth" (1 Kings 17:24).

Missionary, this is a major purpose of our brook-drying experiences. Brook-drying, widow-orphan seasons of life can increase our faith in God's ability to provide and care for us. It also sets the stage for God to show his stuff to an unbelieving audience.

Learn to value rather than despise the dry brooks in your life. Remember, when you're in the valley of the shadow of death, God will never leave you or forsake you. He prepares a table for you in the presence of your enemies. He will walk with you through your valley of the shadow of death. His goodness and mercy will follow you all the days of your life (Psalms 23, paraphrased).

Considerations

1. How's your brook looking?

2. How does God supply you through your brooks, ravens, and widows?

3. What's your next step?

4. What opportunities does your dry brook offer?

(22)

Vicarious Trauma

"Heartache purged layers of baggage I didn't know I carried. Gifts hide under the layers of grief."

Shauna L. Hoey

Elijah's exchanges between the prophet and the people marked an extremely desperate time in the prophet's life. Ever been there?

When I read 1 Kings 17-19 during my initial diagnosis with PTSD—and in the light of my past missionary experiences—, it produced unique applications of this narrative for my personal healing.

Wear and tear. Always on the move, Elijah continually fundraised. He preached a message that most rejected. He often witnessed traumatic events that included suffering and dying people. Watching evil men slaying others in wars and tumults took its toll. In

2 Kings 1, fire consumed two groups of fifty soldiers and their captains before Elijah's very eyes. Ever seen anyone die by fire? It's something you can't put out of your mind.

Influencing the prophets of Baal. 1 Kings 18 cite Elijah's exchange with the prophets of Baal.

> So Ahab summoned all the people of Israel and the prophets to Mount Carmel. Then Elijah stood in front of them and said, "How much longer will you waver, hobbling between two opinions? If the Lord is God, follow him! But if Baal is God, then follow him!" But the people were completely silent. (1 Kings 18:20-21)

Elijah's words presented an exclusive faith. His words and actions were Old Testament. The gospel is exclusive, too. Christ's message is one of grace, hope, and love, and is offered to those who enter the door through faith (John 10:9-16).

Jesus clearly taught his disciples, "I am the way, the truth, and the life. No one can come to the Father except through me" (John 14:6).

In this age of universalism—the idea that all roads lead to God—, an exclusive gospel of faith in Jesus Christ is often not popular. However, let us be careful in making Christ's gospel something that it is not. Christ defined exclusivity as being in him, not in us.

I've met born-again Catholics. Their faith is as firmly rooted in Jesus Christ as that of many Baptists I've known. Yet they remain faithful Catholics.

Now, some of my Baptist friends will recoil at that statement. However, as someone who was raised a Catholic—who still values some aspects of his Catholicism—I offer a caution.

Evangelicals who've never set foot in a Catholic church nor enjoyed the company of Catholic friends should caution themselves as labeling Catholics as "unsaved, lost people" or as "Mary worshippers." I've known a lot of Baptists who were unable to give a single assurance of their salvation outside their baptism, church attendance, and religious activities.

You've heard of Messianic Jews? Not many evangelical Christians question the validity of a Messianic Jew's faith in Jesus Christ.

So are you surprised to learn that there are Messianic Muslims? Yes, there are Muslims who are still Muslims who've placed their faith in Christ. Impossible, you say?

I've met several Messianic Muslims over the years during our time in South Africa. They faithfully go to mosque, follow the precepts of the Koran, but quietly place their trust in Jesus Christ and study the Scriptures. Many of them have found Christ through a series of dreams.

So, Don, you may ask: Are you a Universalist? Not at all! Christ is the way. However, many missionaries realize that when people enter a relationship with Christ, they don't by means of faith break off all identification with their culture any more than do American Christians who still observe Thanksgiving, Christmas, the 4th of July, family traditions, and the like.

> Let us as missionaries not create exclusivities as conditions for inclusion into a faith that Christ did not support.

Let us as missionaries not create exclusivities as conditions for inclusion into a faith that Christ did not support. There is only one condition: "Faith in Jesus Christ." Christ is our banner.

This condition alone brings the scorn of many upon us. We suffer because of Jesus's name. Christ told us this would be so. He warned us of the trauma of proclaiming Christ's message. He said:

> I have come to set the world on fire, and I wish it were already burning! I have a terrible baptism of suffering ahead of me, and I am under a heavy burden until it is accomplished. Do you think I have come to bring peace to the earth? No, I have come to divide

people against each other! From now on families will be split apart, three in favor of me, and two against—or two in favor and three against. (Luke 12:49-52)

A word that describes these words of Jesus is "trauma." Soul-trauma occurs with some missionaries when the message of hope they share is continually rejected. Many missionaries share their discouragement. One missionary wept and said, "What difference does it make? They won't listen. They can care less about Jesus. Let 'em do as they've always done. It's a waste of time."

Once, while out in a Zulu village of forty thousand in the mountains of Natal, South Africa, I stopped at a small store on the outskirts of the village to purchase a soda. As I entered the store, the Indian Muslim store owner screamed at me, "Why don't you leave these people alone?" pointing at Zulu customers standing in line.

My initial thought was, "Yeah, just like you do charging these people three times the price for items they could purchase in town."

God got the best of me as I calmly replied, "I am a guest of several families in this village with whom I've got an appointment. They invited me to dinner. Thanks for your concern." Although he had a scornful sneer on his face, I purchased my soda and gently left the store.

Elijah's message? "Baal won't help you. There's only one hope in this life and the next. That hope is in the Lord God יְהוָה Yĕhovah." Elijah's message of faith stood in direct contrast to the followers of Baal, who encompassed most of society in Elijah's day. Such is the situation many missionaries find themselves today.

Christ's gospel divides, unfortunately. When sharing Christ among other religious contexts, it's necessary to do so with respect for people, their beliefs, and practices. Let Christ be the dividing point. Not you.

Does it surprise you to learn that the great Adoniram Judson built a Zayat (or "meditation place"), which Buddhist teachers used to teach and debate with passersby? He even visited a Buddhist service to learn how the meetings were conducted.[75,76] He avoided direct affronts to either the emperor or the Buddhist religion.[77,78] He adopted the customs and ways of thinking of the Burmese. This enabled him to think as they thought.[79,80,81]

I think that many conservative evangelicals and fundamentalists today might accuse Adoniram Judson of syncretism. Yet, far too often gospel presentations resemble more of a punch in the mouth than a conversation of hope.

> Then Elijah called to the people, "Come over here!" They all crowded around him as he repaired the altar of the Lord that had been torn down. (1 Kings 18:30)

Seeing a person put their faith in Christ is still one of my highest pleasures to witness. Elijah encouraged the people to turn from Baalism—a practice that burned children alive—and embrace the one true God. Mass numbers of people turned to Yĕhovah that day. Imagine the reaction of denominational Baal leaders.

Then Elijah did something God did not command him to do. Elijah took matters into his own hands a bit. A blood bath ensued. Notice:

> Then Elijah commanded, "Seize all the prophets of Baal. Don't let a single one escape!" So the people seized them all, and Elijah took them down to the Kishon Valley and killed them there. (1 Kings 18:40)

Very little is written—that I can find—about the trauma caused by Elijah through witnessing such carnage. Have you ever seen someone hacked to pieces? I'll never get over it.

Perhaps we tend to over-spiritualize Elijah's slaying of the prophets of Baal. His actions afterward, however, show the negative effects of such trauma upon the human soul.

Recently, archeological discoveries revealed surprising data about trauma in Elijah's day. People struggled then with exposure to traumatic events just as do people now.

Assyrian medical texts reveal that people suffered mental trauma and post-traumatic stress due to their harsh environments or exposures to the results of violence, unrest, and war.[82] One ancient text records of a traumatized warrior:

> If in the evening, he sees either a living person or a dead person or someone known to him or someone not known to him or anybody or anything and becomes afraid; he turns around but, like one who has [been hexed with?] rancid oil, his mouth is seized so that he is unable to cry out to one who sleeps next to him."[83]

Another text says:

> They described hearing and seeing ghosts talking to them, who would be the ghosts of people they'd killed in battle—and that's exactly the experience of modern-day soldiers who've been involved in close hand-to-hand combat."[84]

When the first of two Christian therapists diagnosed me with PTSD, my first response was, "That's impossible. I'm not a soldier." As we unfolded the layers of years of experiences in South Africa, numerous episodes of human trauma showed a different picture. Once, as I shared, a vet responded, "Don, okay, you've not been in the military, but, hey, you've seen enough. You've witnessed too much. You're one of us."

Let's remember that God never gave Elijah a command to murder all the prophets of Baal. That was not his ministry, nor is it ours. Yet exposures to the depravities of human nature puts many missionaries in a constant context of human suffering and exploitation. It can and does take a toll to various degrees depending upon a person's inner coping mechanisms to handle such situations.

Traumatized People Affect a Missionary Soul

It was a horrible mess trying to find Wiseman's little baby girl at the hospital morgue after she died of AIDS.

When the morgue door opened, bodies upon bodies laid stacked upon each other. Many died that week. Families struggled to pay for funeral services to collect their loved ones at the hospital.

As the door was opened, the smell was horrendous. I'll never forget it. Neither can I forget the unstacking of the bodies till we found Wiseman's little one at the bottom of that pile of corpses, crushed almost beyond recognition. The whole experience seared my soul. It changed me forever. What's one to do when experiencing such trauma?

Create Some Boundaries

Missionary, you don't need to wade into every human experience of suffering. As you try to alleviate the pain of one person after another, exposure of one's self to multiple traumas on a regular basis impacts the soul and mind. Like Elijah, we are not indestructible.

> Exposure to long-term, repeated trauma can carry devastating effects. Like Elijah, we are not indestructible.

Create necessary protections for your own soul-care and mental health. Take a break occasionally. Exposure to long-term, repeated trauma carries devastating effects.[85] Good self-care requires periods of absence and alleviation from trauma.

When I left South Africa due to my mental health, I remember thinking, "I'm broken. I can't do this any longer. I'm finished." Now I'm healthy, and, looking back, the constant strain of overexposure to death, dying, and suffering proved to have been my Elijah experience.

Talk with Someone

This is difficult. Who does a missionary find to talk with about such things? It's not easy to discuss in the first place. We tend to pack our negative traumatic experiences into the deepest parts of our souls and minds. Transparently sharing our nightmares and fears is not only painful, but it also makes one vulnerable. However, it's worth the risk.

Find someone trustworthy to discuss your traumas with. An empathetic listener. Make it a matter of prayer. It wasn't until beginning to ask God for such people that those people entered my life.

Seek Professional Help if Necessary

Seeking professional help may seem unspiritual, like you're lacking faith. My greatest fear was that knowledge of my condition might hinder me from becoming a missionary again. I was pastoring in northern Minnesota at the time.

My Christian doctor looked at me and said, "Don, if that's what it takes to get you the help you need, wouldn't it be worth it?"

Also, there are costs involved. Talk with your missions agency. Ask God to meet your financial needs.

Today, it's because of God's working in my weaknesses that we—Kathy and I—serve as missionaries to missionaries. God uniquely prepared us through suffering to enter this new ministry. Thank you, God.

Considerations

1. Have you counted such a cost?

2. What's your plan to deal with the trauma you'll possibly experience out there on the field?

3. Have you received any trauma training?

4. Who are you going to talk to?

(23)

Elijah's Cave

Healing and Restoration

Baal worship involved the worship of many deities, but primarily two: Marduk, the champion of the gods, and Tiamat, goddess of the salt sea. Marduk, who was male, and Tiamat, who was female, waged war against other gods for a variety of vengeful reasons.[86]

The religion was also rife with sexual overtones and practices. Elijah's calling sought to bring Israel away from such practices and back to God, to a purer worship of Yahweh. Elijah's message proclaimed the one true God.[87]

Missionaries should seek to proclaim a true faith in the one true Way. For a Christian missionary, hope is found in Jesus Christ (John 14:6). This exclusivity of Jesus's gospel is not readily received in many places. This was true in Jesus's day, too.

In some places, the Way is met with animosity and martyrdom. Graham Stewart Stains and his two sons experienced this to the extreme when five Hindu militants burned them alive in their van in Manoharpur, India, in 1999.[88]

Elijah met such animosity. In 1 Kings 18, after an exhausting stretch of ministry, arguably the greatest prophet of Israel crashed and burned at the height of his prophetic career. In a dark, secluded cave, he threw in the towel. Have you ever been there?

Notice Elijah's state of mind once he entered his cave.

He had just witnessed the pinnacle of ministry. An entire nation looked on as they witnessed a God-miracle at the hands of Elijah. The altar and its contents were consumed by fire falling from the sky. The experience marked a pinnacle of his ministry.

Beware of your mountaintop experiences. To reach such achievements usually marks a period of great exertion physically, emotionally, and spiritually. It is possible that during an all-time high of ministerial experience, one's faculties can also spiral to an all-time low. It's a precarious moment.

He initiated a traumatic event. Elijah—not God—ordered the slaughter of the prophets of Baal. The mental and emotional effects of such carnage upon Elijah are immeasurable. I wonder if Elijah thought much about his actions after the fact. Imagine the trauma of such an event.

He exhausted himself on all levels. A close reading of 1 Kings 18 and 19 indicates a breakneck, continuous schedule. People dying. People denying. People rejoicing. People acting. Missionary, can you relate?

The most powerful leader of the land—Queen Jezebel—threatened his safety. Israel was a dangerous location in which to serve as a prophet. Elijah lived under constant danger. Hazard is a constant companion of many missionaries today, depending upon their location. While living in South Africa, constant trauma and violence produced a wearing-down effect upon all of us.

Despite all his efforts to turn Israel to God, nothing much really changed. Baal worship remained. The people continued to pollute Elijah's message of worshipping the Lord with the religions of the Arkadians and Canaanites. No matter how hard the prophet tried, did anything really change? Did it make a difference? Was it really worth it, or was it just a huge waste of time?

Elijah chooses flight after fight. After confronting the prophets, Elijah recoiled, selecting isolation over engagement. Then came a point in the prophet's life when he tired of the people. Done! Outta here!

Elijah ended up under a broom tree. This sort of reminds one of Jonah. And it's a good name for a tree that literally looks like a broom exuding from the ground. After travelling for hours, Elijah cries under that tree, "God, that's it! Please just let me die now! Kill me!"

Say what? Whoa! Wait a minute, Elijah! How does the great prophet go from confronting the prophets of Baal on Mount Carmel to a weeping, whimpering, whining shadow of a man contemplating suicide?

Sitting next to the bush in the desert, he cries, "Okay, God," sobbing, waah, waah, waah, sniff, sniff, sniff, with a lump in his throat, "Just kill me now. I'm finished. I can't take this any longer!"

Have you never been there? No? Good for you. However, numerous pastors and missionaries share a similar sentiment. Personally, I reached such a place during my last five years in South Africa. Rather than dealing with it, I chose to keep plowing ahead. Ignore. Deny. Rationalize. Spiritualize. Anything but deal with it.

South African friends witnessing my emotional demise suggested returning back "home." But being back home in the American pastorate didn't help. Four years later, I was diagnosed with post-traumatic stress disorder. Trauma and continual exertion took its toll.

You can read more about my journey with PTSD in my book *To Hell, Back, and Beyond – A PTSD Journey: When Faith and Trauma Collide.*

Elijah's Emotions

Elijah's experiences remind us that God created us as emotional creatures. Strong feelings, such as anger, sadness, anxiety, compassion, sympathy, joy, and tenderness, are often instinctive, and we often express emotions physically. This includes increased breathing, rapid heartbeat, tears, laughter, smiles, frowns, and gestures. Emotions may be specific responses to thoughts, actions, or feelings, and emotions are not gender specific. They are messages from our inner self.

Listen to your emotions. Examine them. What causes you to feel or act this way? One missionary shared, "My family says when we arrived back on the field after our furlough, they didn't recognize me any longer. I was a different person." That's a red flag.

Emotions Are Not Facts

Suicidal ideation. Here Elijah contemplated what he believed was his only alternative: suicide. But there are always options other than ending one's life. No situation is without choices. Suicidal ideation is never a good realm to enter into. Get some help if you're at this point.

Overgeneralizing. Elijah scorned his existence. He diminished the prophet's importance and function. His self-denigration reached a new low with thoughts of, "I'm no better than my dead ancestors. I'm no better than dead people. I'm worthless. I'd be more valuable dead than alive."

Moving to Mount Sinai, he entered a cave. There he continued to express negative—but necessary—emotions. This process of expression, while negative in content, was essential to uncovering his issues and moving him toward healing.

Narcissistic. "I have zealously served the Lord God Almighty." He repeated this several times. "I'm doing the right stuff, believing the right way, serving you, God, and what am I getting for all my troubles? Not what I signed up for!" His focus was solely upon himself, his situation, and his perceived past personal accomplishments.

Judgmental. "But the people of Israel have broken their covenant with you, torn down your altars." Question: The people? Who? *All* the people? Every one of them?

Elijah, was there really not one righteous person—hear me now—in the whole country? Not one? You know this to be a fact how? Were you really the only, last one?

Catastrophizing. They've "killed every one of your prophets. I'm the only one left. Now they're trying to kill me too. The very last prophet in *all* of Israel!"

Um, Elijah, what about Obadiah? You spent significant time with him last week. Remember? Yes, some of the prophets were murdered, but you were not the only one left. The situation was difficult to be sure, but it was not hopeless.

Victimization – "I am the only one left. Look how they're treating me. After all I've done for them. They are trying to kill me, too." Me, me, me, and *me*!

Unprocessed Emotions

Elijah seemingly ignored his emotions prior to this rendezvous with God. Allowing unprocessed emotions can cause detrimental developments. When one ignores their emotions, Elijah's cave inevitably follows. Elijah hid his emotions, and a loss of community and crisis of faith followed.

God's Rehabilitation of Elijah

Sleep, Elijah. Elijah, how much rest are you getting? Not much? Here's the thing, Elijah—and all missionaries and pastors—while your calling is supernatural, out of this world, your body still exists in this world. Your body is feeble and fragile if it doesn't meet certain prerequisites.

Life is a temporal existence, encompassed with all kinds of limitations. Don't be so ministry-focused that you overlook the needs of your body. Elijah, go to bed! (1 Kings 19:5-10).

Elijah, what are you eating? You haven't eaten in how long? Get up. Get to the table. Eat a healthy meal. Again, your calling is a spiritual calling, but your body needs food. Good food! It doesn't matter how spiritual your work is. Without a proper diet, you'll be a mess.

Get up! Stretch. Relax. Get proper exercise, Elijah. You can't go, go, go all the time. You're overextending yourself physically.

A therapist friend of mine who works with pastors and missionaries asks almost every client three questions: "What's your sleep like? What do you eat? What's your exercise like?" Sleep, diet, and exercise. He pretty much refuses to work with pastors until he sees improvement in these three areas.

Missionary—I'm entering stormy waters here—, you can't serve God effectively if you're sleep-deprived, one hundred pounds overweight, and void of any exercise.

No, I'm not a fitness guru. I've battled weight most of my adult life. Currently I'm still thirty pounds too heavy. And years of sleep deprivation added to my PTSD woes.

My oldest son, Donnie, remarks even now that I don't eat enough fruits and vegetables. Kathy constantly encourages me to eat less ice cream. My stomach these days demands a severe reduction in dairy anyway. But, oh, how I love ice cream. Especially strawberry cheesecake ice cream!

Living on the road as many missionaries do, which requires eating out all the time, puts on the pounds. (Or kilograms. I used to always cite kilos in my weight gain, and pounds in my weight loss.)

Here's the point: I constantly meet missionaries with a host of physical ailments that have occurred in part due to their lack of sleep, poor diet, and lack of exercise. Take care of yourself. Okay?

Time for respite. An angel told Elijah that a long journey awaited. "You're going to get away for a while, Elijah. Get out of here. There's a place you need to visit. There you'll uncouple yourself from your busy, 'I'm the only prophet left in Israel' —schedule."

"Oh, and while you're there, I've chosen very special accommodations for you. Once you arrive at Mount Sinai, check into the Mount Sinai Cave Hotel. You'll receive instructions from there."

Treatment begins. In the morning, as Elijah awoke in his cave suite, God posed a diagnostic question to this Old Testament missionary. It was profound.

"Elijah, what are you doing here?"

Elijah rehearsed his story, mixed with truth, distortions, and nontruths. It marked a beginning session with God. Perhaps Elijah's greatest distortion was his pragmatic agnosticism.

Elijah obviously believed in God. However, his dialogue with the Lord revealed a false belief that God didn't seem to care or value Elijah's situation. That's called agnosticism.

Missionary, pastor, staff member: have you ever reached such a point, such a faith crisis, in your life? My personal experience and many conversations with missionaries and pastors over the years attests that some—maybe many—reach such a place during their ministries.

The harsh reality is that sometimes we pastors and missionaries, after years of service, transform into unbelieving, God-questioning entities. We become practicing agnostics, preaching something we no longer truly believe.

The grind of ministry, constant exposure to people, minimal solitude, poor spiritual disciplines, pace of schedules, and poor self-talk reduces us into practicing doubters.

God, look at everything I'm doing. *Do you really care?* Then why…? As Elijah asked: "Where are you God? Do you care at all?"

One of the great encouragements of this entire exchange between Elijah and God in 1 Kings 19 is the Lord's response to the ailing prophet and his patience and care for him.

Rather than denounce him, criticize him, fix him, or pontificate to him through a condescending, judgmental approach, God begins with a six-pronged approach to restoration to bring Elijah back to health.

1. **Retreat** – Mount Sinai, a cave, a mountain, and God. Sometimes it's best to pull completely away from the situation for a short time. Rest the brain, gain perspective, and change your thought processing. Refresh your soul.

2. **Refocus** – Self-talk often becomes a destructive element when seeded in distortions and mistruths. Here, viewing the majesty of the mountains, Elijah begins moving away from his anxieties. He begins talking with God instead of with himself. He gains more of a God-perspective than a self-perspective.

3. **Reason** – What is really happening in your life, Elijah? You place a lot of emphasis on things, events, and people. What's

really going on here? Where are you, Elijah? Where is your God?

    a. Stop looking to the wind.
    b. Stop looking to the earthquake.
    c. Stop looking to the fire.
    d. Just look to me: your God.

4. **Reconsider** – Elijah. Listen. Shush. Be quiet. Just listen, Elijah. Cast all those anxieties away. Stop looking for God in performances, programs, and people. I, God, am right here. I've always been here with you. I've never left you.

5. **Redirect** – "Elijah, what are you doing here?" Besides these recorded words, one wonders what else God said to Elijah. Maybe more, maybe not, but a significant change occurs during this interaction based upon the next recorded words of God.

6. **Revitalize** – "Elijah, get up and go out. Get cracking again. I've got a ton of important things for you to do. You're fit, rested, healthy, and focused on me again. Now get going."

We all need an Elijah's cave or two in our lives. It's during our cave-dwelling intimacies with God and ourselves that our souls can emerge from the grotto in deeper faith and redirection.

Embrace your cave. No matter how dark or deep that cave is, listen for God. Then listen *to* God. Get the help you need, then help yourself. Get healthy. Then move forward again in faith. Read Hebrews 11:6 over and over again, especially the last sentence. I know you know the verse, it's just that you really don't *know* this verse. Hebrews 11:6 helped me emerge from my cave.

> And it is impossible to please God without faith. Anyone who wants to come to him must believe that God exists and that he **rewards those who sincerely seek him**. (emphasis added)

Sincerely seeking God helped me step out from my cave leading me to where we—Kathy and myself—are today. Trauma drove me into the cave, but God and his people led me out of it into meaningful purpose and worth.

Missionary, please hear me now. I know many missionaries from dozens of agencies. One of the great, untold stories of missionaries is the number of them whose seared souls drove them into their caves, never to resurface again.

Don't become that missionary. Recognize when you need help, and ask for it—get it. Don't waste your pain dwelling in a cave indefinitely berating, begrudging, and bellowing your bad fortune. It's a lousy place to live. Pain can serve a greater purpose than that. It can propel you toward God and greater service.

> See God in your cave. Don't waste your pain. Allow pain to drive you closer to God. Find purpose in your trauma.

Don't waste your pain.

Considerations

1. What about you?

2. What about your trauma?

3. What are you doing to deal with your trauma?

4. How can you see God in your cave?

5. Who you going to talk to?

Leaving an Elisha Legacy

I once heard a pastor who was preaching on Elijah's life make an interesting statement. He said, "After Elijah cried in the cave, 'God, that's it, I quit,' you never hear from him again. God never used him again. So we must never quit."

The problem with that statement is that it's wildly inaccurate. In fact, Elijah's cave produced a prophet who went on to see his greatest accomplishment in the last eight years of his life: his protégé, the prophet Elisha.

God Has Appointed Your Elisha

One of the great narratives on the virtues of mentorship occur in Elijah and Elisha's exchanges. Standing just outside the cave, Elijah receives instructions from God to find the young, arrogant prophet name Elisha. Elijah is to anoint him as his replacement. That process will take eight years to accomplish.

Younger and Older Prophets Are Starkly Different

There was quite a difference between the older prophet and the younger, rookie prophet candidate.

The older Elijah acted mostly as a solitary figure. Aloof, he showed up on the scene often unannounced and unexpected. Elisha, on the other hand, was often seen in the "School of the Prophets," interacting and socializing with his students training to become prophets. Elisha lived in community, whereas Elijah lived primarily in solitude (1 Kings 18:43-44; 2 Kings 4:43; 5:8, 10, 9:1-3).[89]

Elijah is better known among the two prophets, but Elisha was far more active.

Elijah was stern, hard, and unbending.

Elisha was friendly and interactive.

Most of Elijah's miracles were works of judgement.

Many of Elisha's miracles assisted people in need.

Elisha allowed the Aramean soldiers to return to their land in safety, whereas Elijah let fire consume those who sought to apprehend him (2 Kings 1:9-12, 6:21-23).[90]

Although Elisha patterned some of his miraculous acts after those of his mentor Elijah, in many ways their prophetic styles differed. Each prophet was distinctive, bringing a special message and approach to his role.[91]

I don't know about you, but Elijah sounds like many—no, most—older, boomer missionaries today, while Elisha bears many similar traits to younger millennials missionaries.

Mentoring Elisha—Our Greatest Task

Older missionary, your greatest asset is the Elishas you leave behind. As your name and work fade in the rearview mirror of life—

and they will—, those staying after your departure will determine your ministry's real success. It's not in the buildings or structures you leave behind, but rather in the Elishas you've left to carry on the work.

Too many times—way too many—, missionaries leave the field only to see their works close shop and shut the doors. Sometimes such progressions are natural. There is a life cycle to every ministry. Other times, the failure of the work is directly attributable to an absence of a strong, mature Elisha.

In South Africa, some of our ministries remain in the hands of wonderful, dedicated African people. One center alone boasts dozens of medical staff personnel, teachers, and counselors. All of whom are paid for and staffed by South Africans.

Some ministries suffer closures because they experience a leadership crisis. People are sheep; without leaders, they wander aimlessly.

The Elisha you mentor today can become your legacy tomorrow. Then, Elijah, you can take the back seat and let your Elisha fly high. Don't (as I've sometimes seen done) rip the ministry out of your young Elisha's hands because you are jealously seeking the top spot on the platform again.

Elijah Deserves Your Respect

Younger missionaries, I know that we older, battle-worn missionaries often seem obtuse, impersonal, and unapproachable. That's because many times we are! But please give those crusty, older missionaries your respect. They've earned it. Many times they've witnessed younger missionaries come before you who lasted no longer than a few years.

> Elisha, Elijah deserves your respect. Elijah, Elisha deserves your time. Come together right now over Christ.

In my case, one missionary family lasted only six weeks before retiring back to Missouri, citing a host of made-up excuses.

I've often encouraged younger missionaries struggling under the leadership of an older, seasoned missionary with this question: "What has that older missionary done right to last so many years in missionary service?"

It's easy to criticize. And, yes, we older missionaries can be a stuffy, stubborn, self-righteous lot. However, if a veteran missionary doesn't deserve some respect after learning the language and living thirty years on the field, then who does?

Elijah about the Younger Elishas

This rising generation—often referred to as Generation Y, or millennials—has been characterized as a group of apathetic, unmotivated, and unreliable individuals. However, their many positive aspects may surprise you.[92]

Contrary to coffee talking points today by boomers concerning arrogant, entitled millennials, many younger missionaries bring a host of talents to the mission field.

These tech-savvy, highly interpersonal, multitasking individuals are the highest educated generation in both American history and other countries, too.

Millennials make up thirty-four percent of the global workforce.[93] That number will increase by 2050. Here's my point: As older missionaries move off the scene, younger missionaries will replace us. And, older missionary, we *are* moving off the scene. Don't you want to become part of a wonderful, rewarding venture that develops and provides younger missionaries with great opportunities to grow God's kingdom?

Understand that millennials don't want to waste their lives. They are non-complacent. They won't settle for your ministry; they want their own ministry. Just like I suspect you did when you were their age way back in 1980.

They will not fit into the traditional mold of missions we held to just a few decades ago. They want to make a difference with their lives, not tread the waters of ecclesiastic policies and procedures.

They don't care for the corporate mindset of missions of the past. Many choose to venture out on their own rather than through traditional missionary agencies. Often they will tell you to your face that they don't agree with you.

Be patient. Practice forgiveness. Help them achieve their own success. They wince at working for "the man" when you lean hard on them. Don't be "the man." Be the one who maturely mentors them into greater marriage, family, and missionary success than yours. It takes a big heart full of compassion and forgiveness. Be that mentor.

Remember Jesus's words: "So those who are last now will be first then, and those who are first will be last" (Matthew 20:16).

Be the last so that Jesus becomes the first in life and ministry.

Elisha Wants It All

Notice the request of the younger Elisha. He demanded, "Please let me inherit a double share of your spirit and become your successor" (2 Kings 2:9). Wow! The arrogance! Twice as much? What a punk! What an entitled little brat. You want to be twice as great as me? Who do you think you are?

Here's a secret: It's not about you. It's about making God a big deal. Not you, Elijah. Or, even you, Elisha.

What was Elijah's response? "If that's God's will, it will be so." Now there's a great, mature missionary. "I'll walk with you on God's journey in your life. I hope you do more, influence more, and leave more in your ministry than do I."

Let us remember, God is at work. Some pioneer the work, some implement it, others refine it, and some manage it, but God gives the increase. It's God's kingdom. It's Christ's church.

Elijah, here's your number one question: How can you help that young Elisha succeed at whatever God has called him or her to do?

And, Elisha, here's a question for you: What can you learn from your mentor missionary that can make the difference between a productive, enduring missionary service and early departure?

It Takes Two to Leave a Legacy

Both boomer and millennial missionaries require a bond of mutual respect, integrity, and trust. Elijahs, take the fledgling Elishas under your wings. They are your legacy.

The younger Elisha submitted to the older prophet's leadership. In many ways he was the complete opposite of Elijah, but together they influenced the kingdoms of Israel and Judah. Together, for God, they moved forward in God's calling.

Elisha, learn everything you can from those ancient missionaries you meet upon arriving on your field. Their greatest asset might be the simple fact that they've survived.

Elijah, what about you? When your chariot takes you out of this world, what will you leave behind? Struggling remnants of your ministry's remains? Or an Elisha or two who takes the work beyond the capabilities of your influence?

Leave an Elisha legacy. Anything else becomes just a diminishing memory.

Considerations

1. What Elishas are you mentoring?

2. Who are you going to pour your life into?

3. How do you relate to younger or older missionaries?

4. What does your legacy look like?

(25)

The Art of Leaving Well

Within the pages of this chapter, I share what is probably my greatest failure as a missionary. It's a failure that enough missionaries make that some missionary agencies developed guidelines for their missionary personnel when they depart for the field.

Not leaving the field well can produce stress all the way around for everyone. As many missionaries share, reentry into your country of birth often proves more difficult than one's first arrival to the field. This was particularly true for me.

In the book of Acts, chapter 20, an account of a good missionary farewell occurs.

Paul, during his departure from Roman Christians at Ephesus, gives us a good model to follow.

Departures are distressing for everyone. Here in Acts 20:37-38 in the Amplified Bible, the language of distress is much harsher than what is found in many other English translations.

> And they began to weep openly and threw their arms around Paul's neck, and repeatedly kissed him, grieving and distressed

especially over the word which he had spoken, that they would not see him again. And they accompanied him to the ship.

To this day I regret not taking the time to properly say farewell to several close individuals in South Africa upon our departure. In the busyness of departure, some individuals got overlooked. Since some of those individuals now reside in heaven, I desire forgiveness from them when we meet in heaven one day.

Take the necessary time to show as much love in your departure as you did in your enthusiastic arrival. Depart with the consistency of the compassion you proclaimed during your years on the field.

Rehearse God's blessings of ministry together. Paul rehearsed the good, the bad, and the ugly of serving God with the Ephesian leaders. Their challenges and victories reflected their deep bond. Paul's focus was on God's mutual call in all their lives—not just God's latest moving in Paul's life.

Make your departure about Christ. Paul emphasized, "I have had one message for Jews and Greeks alike—the necessity of repenting from sin and turning to God, and of having faith in our Lord Jesus" (Acts 20:21).

One of the highest pinnacles of success for a missionary is when Christ, not the missionary, is Lord in the hearts of the people. Make much about Christ, and less about yourself. Remember:

> Therefore, God elevated him to the place of highest honor
>   and gave him the name above all other names,
> that at the name of Jesus every knee should bow,
>   in heaven and on earth and under the earth,
> and every tongue declare that Jesus Christ is Lord,
>   to the glory of God the Father (Philippians 2:9-11).

Make much of God in your future. In Acts 20:22, Paul gave details of his new, anticipated ministry. His words left no doubt of the

Holy Spirit's leading, when he said, "And now I am bound by the Holy Spirit to go to Jerusalem."

It's much easier to accept that the missionary is departing because of God's leading. This presents a positive contrast to the missionary's fatigue of the current location or excitement for adventure in another, newer place.

Leave a dedication rather than a regret. In his departure, Paul continued the process of sanctification. He said,

> And now I entrust you to God and the message of his grace that is able to build you up and give you an inheritance with all those he has set apart for himself (Acts 20:32).

Let mutual prayer and blessings be your last words. After they prayed together, they said the final farewells.

One of my great regrets is Duduzi. Duduzi was a young Zulu man I led to Jesus Christ thirty years ago. He grew into a leader, pastoring one of our churches in a place named Ezakheni, in Ladysmith, South Africa.

In my departure, a final farewell between the two of us got lost in the shuffle. I was unable to locate him on social media, and none of my attempts to reconnect met with success.

Leaving well encourages a good reentry into your home country, too. Tie up your loose ends. Honor the people you've served. Above all, honor the God who called you in the first place.

(26)

"Q"

Six months after leaving South Africa, I sat in my office in Eagan, Minnesota. As the new pastor in this suburban church, the American pastorate posed new challenges for me.

On a particular day, a visitor sat unannounced across from me at my desk. Several churches in the greater Twin Cities area financially supported us during our many years in South Africa. This pastor represented a church that had supported our ministry with twenty-five dollars per month.

He said, "Man, you really let us down."

"Let who down?" I replied.

"Me and pastor M_____," he replied.

Pastor M's church had supported us with seventy-five dollars per month for a number of our missionary years.

I inquired, "How did I let you down?"

"Well, we supported you all those years in South Africa, and then you just quit. If we'd known you were a quitter, we'd never have supported you. It's just another big 'Q' for our missions program."

That "ticked my dander just a wee little bit," as a Scottish friend in South Africa often said.

I responded, "Well, get in line. Is there anything else I can help you with?"

Our exchange ended shortly thereafter.

The next day, another pastor from a previously supportive church in Indiana phoned me. He said, "Don, I just want to thank you and Kathy for your years of service representing our church in South Africa. Welcome home."

Wow! That turned my mood into more positive—not wanting to knock-a-pastor-out—attitude.

Fast-forward ten years later. Kathy and I were missionaries again and traveling from church to church raising our support.

We sat with an influential pastor and his wife at lunch. The pastor asked, "So, the first time you were a missionary, why did you quit?"

I thought, "Well, this is the third church you've pastored. Did you quit the other two?" My mind started to contemplate thoughts like, "Why expect missionaries to do that which you'd never contemplate doing on your most self-righteous day?"

I can be quite an internally grumpy guy sometimes. I think it's the passive-aggressive Minnesota thing in me. Or maybe it's just that I'm a fallen, sin-laden human being just like everyone else.

Thankfully, the Holy Spirit got the better of me. I replied, "Pastor, I didn't resign; God reassigned me."

But those words did not congeal his premeditative judgement. Lunch finished, and I knew we'd never hear from him again. His mind was made up that I was a quitter.

His final words were, "Keep in touch." Loosely translated, that meant, "Don't ever call again."

Driving out of the parking lot, Kathy said, "He thinks you're a quitter. He just can't understand." I thought, "No, he doesn't *want* to understand."

That pastor? Well, he's a good man. He's built a solid church. He's just as much a son of God as myself. Many pastors are generous, genuine people. They treat us very well.

But it's by the few negative experiences that we tend to remember and classify all people. Don't we? We as missionaries must avoid this.

Most pastors are understanding, caring folk. They just don't possess enough margin of time to allow you to adequately explain your circumstances for leaving your field. And, for many, they will never get it. It's simply not on their radar.

Reassigned, Not Resigned

Your attitude concerning your return from the field defines you more than others. Not your actual return, but how you view yourself. You express more about yourself than others. It also engenders an attitude of how others perceive you.

Missionary, you've been reassigned, not resigned. Don't wear that shameful "Q," because it doesn't represent you. Release the shameful "Q" about your neck. A cowering, quitting demeanor shadows your presence and sets your tone for reentry.

> Missionary, you've been reassigned, not resigned. Don't wear "Quitter" on your person.

Think about this for a moment. What did you do during your time on the mission field? Share Christ? Share his gospel? Do the good works you were created to do in Christ Jesus (Ephesians 2:8-10)? Did you resign from this? No, missionaries never leave what God created us to become in him through his son, Jesus Christ.

Going back home is a reassignment of continuing that which God created you to do in the first place, regardless of geographical location. Please don't resign from loving him, loving others, and influencing people for Christ. You're the same person in Christ regardless of whether you live here or there.

Thank God for His Calling

Thank God for calling you to your past field of service. Thank God for reassigning you now to a new field of service. If you are recuperating—which is a vital necessity for missionaries—, then thank God for his plans to open opportunities to heal you and move you forward.

He who began the good missionary work in you will be faithful to complete it. Fear not. Fret not. Forget not. Move forward.

Pat Yourself on the Back

If you spent much time on the mission field serving as a career missionary, you are ahead of the majority of pastors I know. Their trips usually last only a week or two every other year or so. They serve in their own mission fields in the communities of the churches they pastor.

The fact is, you've spent more time on the mission field than probably most your supporters collectively.

You've got nothing about which to hang your head in shame. Stand tall. You've lived in another country and culture for many years. You've learned another language. How many people ever do that? How many come close to touching your experiences?

Pat yourself on the back with your fortune. You've lived in a way that few have or can contemplate. Don't let others sully your experiences. Don't denigrate your missionary life.

Change that "Q" of quitter to a "Q" of quest. Your journey has taken you too far and wonderful places and back again. You're a world explorer, returned to familiar shore.

Welcome home.

(27)

Reentry – Check Your Expectations

Some missionaries share that reentry into their country of birth was more difficult than beginning to live in a distant field. Such stories are not uncommon. Missionaries possess expectations upon their return to family and friends. This challenge is not a new development in our modern era. Missionaries one hundred years ago shared similar disappointments with their reentries to their countries of birth.

> An old missionary couple worked in Africa for years, and they were returning to New York City to retire.
>
> They enjoyed no pension; their health was broken; they were defeated, discouraged, and afraid.
>
> They discovered they were booked on the same ship as President Teddy Roosevelt, who was returning from one of his big-game hunting expeditions.

No one paid much attention to them. They watched the fanfare that accompanied the president's entourage, with passengers trying to catch a glimpse of the great man.

As the ship moved across the ocean, the old missionary said to his wife, "Something is wrong. Why should we have given our lives in faithful service for God in Africa all these many years and have no one care a thing about us?

Here this man comes back from a hunting trip and everybody makes much over him, but nobody gives two hoots about us."[94]

His wife cautioned him that he should not feel this way. Henry replied, "I know, but I just can't help it. It just isn't right."

His wife then said, "Henry, you know God doesn't mind if we honestly question Him. You need to tell this to the Lord and get this settled now. You'll be useless in His ministry until you do."

Henry Morrison began pouring out his heart to the Lord. "Lord, you know our situation and what's troubling me. We gladly served you faithfully for years without complaining. But now, God, I just can't get this incident out of my mind..."

Henry returned to the living room with a peaceful look on his face. His wife said, "It looks like you've resolved the matter. What happened?"

Henry replied, "The Lord settled it for me. I told him how bitter I was that the president received this tremendous homecoming, but no one even met us as we returned home. When I finished, it seemed as though the Lord put his hand on my shoulder and simply said, 'But, Henry, you are not home yet!'"[95]

Can you relate? How many were present at your send-off to the field? How many welcomed you back upon your resignation/return?

Upon reentry to your country of origin, understand that you've changed and your family, friends, and colleagues have changed, too. And in your return, people's perceptions of you changed again. You now exist between two cultures.

In-between Cultured People

We become what I like to call "in-between cultured people." Entering and living in a new culture during our adult years marks a difference between us and a MK or TCK.

Upon my return to Minnesota, my struggle to understand the perceived trivial existence of most American Christians marked my deeper worldview. It also pointed to a judgmental spirit on my part.

People talked about their domestic pets, traffic, and recreation. This was meaningless drivel to me. It all seemed incredibly frivolous.

Interestingly, I've shared very little of my world travels and experiences with most American friends, family, and foes as they don't really care to hear about such things. They are too busy talking about themselves to listen to others.

Twelve years after returning to the United States, America still does not feel like home. I've learned to navigate through conversations here, but mentally I struggle to connect. Like Abraham leaving his home of Ur, I'm a wanderer finding settling down into any one place difficult, if not impossible.

Prayer meetings present a great example. In South Africa, our Zulu members prayed for enough food to feed their children during the week, or for the strength to walk ten miles to work and back again each day, since they were unable to afford the fare to take the bus.

They prayed for strength to give a good witness for Jesus at the funeral of their child, who was their third child to die.

Women prayed that their husbands, who were returning home for Christmas from the mines in Johannesburg, wouldn't give them the AIDS they contracted from their work-wives.

American prayer meetings centered around healing for Grandma's goiter.

See where I'm going with this?

As an in-between cultured person, it often feels like I'm standing in-between two cultures, struggling to find meaningful conversations, let alone existence.

Yet both walks are legitimate. A faith walk in affluency is just as valid as one in poverty.

Everything's Changed, but Nothing's Changed

People in your country of birth moved on with their lives after you left for your mission field. They forgot about your calling. The longer you're gone, the more distant your relationships become.

When you arrived back home for good, guess what? In their minds, all the missionary stuff matters little. As one told me, "Don, you're not a missionary anymore. Let it go, will yah?"

This realization shocked me upon returning to the United States in 2006.

During our many years in South Africa, the suburbs of the United States exploded. Throughout the entire country, sprawling new communities sprang up.

Traveling back to Minneapolis, Minnesota, my childhood home, everything changed. Almost every house we lived in (and we moved quite often) was gone. So was my grade school. They demolished it to make room for a new school miles away. They tore my middle school down as well. All had changed.

Be ready for those types of changes. Understand:

You changed.
They changed.
Your church changed.
Your culture changed.
Your family changed.
Your friendships changed, too.

Look forward to newness, not the familiar surroundings of your past. They don't exist any longer.

Pitfalls to Avoid

Missionaries share a number of common frustrations upon reentry. Here's just a few of the challenges.

Resentment. Your peers probably possess more than you do. While you spent years raising support, living in a third world country, and serving God, guess what? Your friends bought big houses, new cars, cabins, boats, and a host of other trinkets and toys.

It's easy to feel that while you gave up everything to serve God while other Christians spent their time and energies acquiring lots of fabulous junk for themselves.

Yes, stuff matters, but not that much. Looking at perhaps my last twenty years of life, stuff doesn't seem as important now. We all want nice things, especially we missionaries who lived in impoverished countries. It's reasonable to want something nice.

Let us remember, however, that faith is a life about God, not stuff.

Disillusionment. When you return from the field, not many—if any—will really want to hear about your mission field experiences any more. Why? You're not a missionary any longer. People become acquaintances and friends rather than supporters.

Ron and Bonnie Koteskey, who are member care consultants with Go International, point out: "You return home all excited about what you have been doing, but everyone at home seems so apathetic. As one person put it, 'They are comatose and don't even know it.'"[96]

Here's the truth: They live their lives. You live yours. Life is so full for many that they possess little time for anyone else's life. And here's a question to consider: Why is my missionary life more important than a domesticated Christian's life? (Okay, yes, I confess that smacked of some criticism there.)

One good way to combat this is to thoroughly thank all your supporters. Thank every person individually who prayed for you. Combat your disillusionment with gratitude. It works!

A hypercritical attitude. Some of the most critical people I've ever met are missionaries. I used to be one. You know, a judgmental, "You don't measure up," kind of ex-missionary. You probably don't know much about that kind of feeling, however. Right?

No one sacrificed as much as you did. They don't understand like you do. They not as spiritual as you. Their lives aren't as meaningful as a missionary life. Your personal comparisons to your experiences mark many contrasts with others. Those contrasts can become sources of criticisms of others.

That's called pride. I possessed much of it in those days. One thing that helped was to remember that those I was prone to criticize are just as loved and valued by God as myself. Take a look at the first few verses in Philippians 2.

The angry missionary – Resentment and aggression results when missionaries leave such attitudes unchecked. Most missionaries will experience some level of these emotions.

Missionary, talk to someone. Get some counsel. Give yourself time. Much of what you feel is a natural result of the transition you'll experience. Don't allow anger to replace the good God has done in your life.

Grieve your losses. They are losses. Weep if needed. Jesus wept. It's okay. You're going to struggle with what you're leaving behind and the adjustments ahead. It's okay to hurt. In your hurt, be careful not to hurt others.

Give it time. Understand your new journey. Engage rather than disengage. Remember, the God on your missionary field is the same God in your current journey.

Considerations

1. How much did you change during your time in missionary service?

2. How much did your friends and family change?

3. Which pitfall do you currently struggle with the most?

4. How will you overcome that deficit?

(28)

Well Done!

Sitting in my office in Northern Minnesota, my administrative assistant informed me of a phone call. She said, "Pastor, sorry to bother you, but I think you need to take this call right now." Grudgingly, I answered, "Hello, this is pastor Don."

A sobbing missionary began: "Hello, this is R____ M____. Your church supports us. I'm sorry to inform you that we can't return to our field. We are in Iowa right now. We won't be able to return." A further conversation revealed that his missionary wife suffered from severe agoraphobia. This fear can be so overwhelming that one feels unable to leave their home.[97]

This missionary's wife received a year of treatment but was still unable to leave their rented house in Iowa. Some spiritual leaders around them talked of her affliction as result of "spiritual warfare," a "lack of faith," or a "failure of obedience."

Without compensation, care, or preparation, their missions agency terminated their missionary employment. The missionary—who was also an MK—lost the only life he'd ever known.

After listening for over an hour, I offered, "R_____, thank you for your faithful service. Thanks for putting the needs of your wife above your desire for ministry and missionary work. I don't have a lot of answers, but I know God is faithful. May he show you in some way his purpose in all of this. You're not a failure. You are my hero. God will right all these things one day."

Continuing, I encouraged, "Don't let 'missionary' define who you are. Don't allow your agency to define your quality. Well done for your faithful service! Be encouraged, you're a child of God. Great is your reward in heaven."

With that, he thanked me profusely for our time together. We prayed together and hung up. After speaking with our leadership, our church sent a healthy check to help with their expenses.

Many missionaries who return to their country of birth after their missionary service—whether it be two or thirty years—share a profound sense of failure. I've heard it a hundred times and experienced it myself. With their heads hanging, they say, "We used to be missionaries but . . ."

That "but" speaks unknown volumes.

Missionary, please don't condemn yourself for spending more time in a foreign country sharing Jesus than probably most your supporters combined.

Where in Scripture does it teach that the missionary calling is to a specific place for an entire lifetime?

Celebrate your journey. Don't call "sad" that which God makes glad. Don't sully that which God called you to. Don't allow another to do the same. Be faithful right now. Walk with God every day. In every way. In every place.

Faith is about today. Faith moves forward; faith doesn't look back. Other spiritual qualities do, but not faith. Faith is a forward-moving action toward God, regardless of whether you're in your promised land or on a new journey from Ur of the Chaldees.

Move forward. Don't look back. Keep your eyes on forward horizons, not on the storms of the past. One step in front of the other.

Yes, it's difficult. But this new journey presents opportunities for faith, for maturity to grow. That's what God is all about.

Advance. Keep your eyes on the prize. Then hear the words:

"Well done, my good and faithful servant. You have been faithful in handling this small amount, so now I will give you many more responsibilities. Let's celebrate together!"

Jesus
(Matthew 25:21)

Take a bow. You are my hero.

Should you wish to share thoughts about missionary life, care, or encouragement, please email at missionarytoo@gmail.com

Other books by Don Mingo

To Hell, Back, and Beyond - A PTSD Journey: When Faith and Trauma Collide. Available on Amazon in paperback, Kindle, and Kindle Unlimited.

Son Risings – Discovering and Caring for the Real You. Available on Amazon in paperback, Kindle, and Kindle Unlimited.

Boundaries – 5 Steps to Getting Your Life Back. Helping people overcome pornography addiction with God's help. Faithway Publishers, Available on Amazon in paperback and Kindle.

Life Boundaries – Balancing Career, Marriage, Relationships, and the Important Stuff of Life. Available on Amazon in paperback, Kindle, and Kindle Unlimited.

Get Your Life Back Addiction Workbook. A 21-week addiction workbook. This is virtually the same as Get Your Life Back! Journal.

End Notes

[1] http://www.aboutmissions.org/statistics.html
[2] Wimpy's is my favorite breakfast place in South Africa. The chain is found throughout the country.
[3] Unless otherwise indicated, all Scripture quotations are taken from the Holy Bible, New Living Translation, copyright © 1996, 2004, 2015 by Tyndale House Foundation. Used by permission of Tyndale House Publishers, Inc., Carol Stream, Illinois 60188. All rights reserved.
[4] Sir Walter Scott, "Breathes There the Man."
[5] http://www.dictionary.cambridge.org/us/dictionary/english/expectation
[6] http://www.macmillandictionary.com/us/dictionary/american/expectation
[7] Ibid.
[8] http://www.dictionary.com/browse/expectancy?s=t
[9] http://www.imb.org/2017/09/20/expectations-vs-expectancy-fine-line-missionary-attrition/
[10] Hudson Taylor; *China's Spiritual Need and Claims*, 1865.
[11] https://www.christianitytoday.com/history/issues/issue-52/hudson-taylor-missions-to-china-did-you-know.html
[12] Eugene Myers Harrison, quoted in *Giants of the Missionary Trail*, Chicago: Scripture Press Foundation, 1954, 73
[13] https://www.nytimes.com/1987/11/28/world/for-zimbabwe-missionaries-a-night-of-terror-and-death.html
[14] Andy Johnson, *Missions: How the Local Church Goes Global*, Crossway, 2017.
[15] https://kategillieart.com/ptsd-treatments-and-therapies/
[16] Ibid.
[17] http://withinreachglobal.org/4-truths-to-help-overcome-loneliness-on-the-mission-field/
[18] http://www.biblestudytools.com/commentaries/robertsons-word-pictures/mark/mark-8-32.html
[19] http://nehemiahproject.org/losing-your-soul/
[20] Ibid.
[21] Ibid.
[22] Gesenius's Hebrew and Chaldee Lexicon - Study Resources. Retrieved from https://www.blueletterbible.org/study/lexica/gesenius/index.cfm

[23] Gesenius' Hebrew-Chaldee Lexicon as cited in https://www.blueletterbible.org/lang/lexicon/lexicon.cfm?Strongs=H7462&t=KJV
[24] H3068 - Yĕhovah - Strong's Hebrew Lexicon (KJV).
[25] https://sleepfoundation.org/media-center/press-release/lack-sleep-affecting-americans-finds-the-national-sleep-foundation
[26] http://english.stackexchange.com/questions/14876/use-quotation-marks-or-italics-for-written-quotes
[27] http://tinybuddha.com/blog/are-you-too-busy-5-signs-of-chronic-stress/
[28] https://www.sri.com/work/projects/specific-changes-brain-associated-sleep-deprivation
[29] http://www.thinkhealthmag.com/how-rest-and-relaxation-benefits-you/
[30] http://tvsmarter.com/documents/brainwaves.html
[31] http://motherboard.vice.com/read/is-watching-tv-actually-a-good-way-to-rest-your-brain
[32] http://www.biblestudytools.com/lexicons/hebrew/nas/shuwb.html
[33] https://www.blueletterbible.org/kjv/psa/23/3/p0/t_conc_501003
[34] Don Mingo, *Boundaries: 5 Steps to Getting Your Life Back*.
[35] https://www.lastdaysministries.org/Groups/1000086208/Last_Days_Ministries/Articles/By_Keith_Green/Everything_You_Should/Everything_You_Should.aspx

[36] https://www.desiringgod.org/articles/sexual-sin-in-the-ministry
[37] https://www.imdb.com/title/tt0499549/quotes
[38] https://www.crossculture.com/about-us/the-model/
[39] http://www.businessinsider.com/the-lewis-model-2013-9
[40] Ibid.
[41] Ibid.
[42] https://www.crossculture.com/wp-content/uploads/2014/09/World_Linear-active.png
[43] https://www.crossculture.com/wp-content/uploads/2014/09/World_Multi-active.png
[44] http://www.exactlywhatistime.com/other-aspects-of-time/time-in-different-cultures/
[45] https://online.seu.edu/high-and-low-context-cultures/
[46] Ibid.
[47] https://www.asme.org/engineering-topics/articles/business-communication/communicating-across-cultures (reprinted from the

website of the American Management Association at www.amanet.org).
[48] Ibid.
[49] Ibid.
[50] https://www.challies.com/articles/shame-fear-guilt/
[51] Ibid.
[52] https://www.cleveland.com/metro/index.ssf/2017/10/rocky_river_dad_admits_to_kill.html
[53] https://www.challies.com/articles/shame-fear-guilt/
[54] https://dornsife.usc.edu/assets/sites/782/docs/oysermancoonkemmelmeier2002.pdf
[55] Ibid.
[56] *Psychological Bulletin*, 2002, American Psychological Association, Inc., Vol. 128, No. 1, 3–72, https://dornsife.usc.edu/assets/sites/782/docs/oysermancoonkemmelmeier2002.pdf.
[57] https://www.slideshare.net/uncstaff/individualism-collectivism-high-and-low-context
[58] Ibid.
[59] Ibid.
[60] https://www.slideshare.net/uncstaff/individualism-and-collectivism
[61] Clement Clarke Moore, *A Visit from St. Nicholas*, Public Domain.
[62] https://www.thegospelcoalition.org/article/the-number-one-reason-missionaries-go-home/
[63] http://www.alifeoverseas.com/is-conflict-with-teammates-really-the-top-reason-for-missionaries-leaving-the-field/
[64] https://www.discprofile.com/what-is-disc/overview/
[65] http://www.discoveryreport.com/DISC-and-MBTI-Myers-Briggs-Type-Indicator.html
[66] https://www.christianitytoday.com/history/people/missionaries/hudson-taylor.html
[67] https://www.christianitytoday.com/history/issues/issue-56/paradox-of-david-livingstone-did-you-know.html
[68] Wayland Francis, *A Memoir of the Life and Labors of the Rev. Adoniram Judson*, Volume 1, 1853, 33

[69] Rick Corum, *Principles of Management: A Christian Perspective*, WestBow Press, 2015.

[70] http://www.alifeoverseas.com/an-open-letter-to-parents-of-missionary-kids/
[71] http://www.alifeoverseas.com/an-open-letter-to-parents-of-missionary-kids/
[72] https://www.imdb.com/title/tt0694856/quotes
[73] https://www.mayoclinic.org/healthy-lifestyle/adult-health/in-depth/empty-nest-syndrome/art-20047165
[74] https://baptistnews.com/article/southern-baptists-to-cut-missionary-force-by-15-percent/#.W0Xj-9JKjIU
[75] https://theologicalstudies.org.uk/article_judson.html#56
[76] Anderson, Courtney, *To The Golden Shore: The Life of Adoniram Judson*, Valley Forge: Judson Press, 1987, 220.
[77] https://theologicalstudies.org.uk/article_judson.html#56
[78] Anderson, 236.
[79] https://theologicalstudies.org.uk/article_judson.html#60
[80] Ruth Tucker, *From Jerusalem To Irian Jaya*, Grand Rapids: Zondervan, 1983, 121; Anderson, 128.
[81] Anderson, 312.
[82] https://www.ancient-origins.net/news-history-archaeology/weapons-and-tactics-change-ptsd-goes-back-millennia-002613
[83] Ibid.
[84] https://www.smithsonianmag.com/smart-news/ancient-assyrian-soldiers-were-haunted-war-too-180954022/
[85] https://theoakstreatment.com/blog/ctsd-continuous-traumatic-stress-disorder/
[86] https://en.wikipedia.org/wiki/Tiamat
[87] http://www.crivoice.org/baal.html
[88] http://www.cnn.com/WORLD/asiapcf/9901/23/india.christian/index.html
[89] https://www.thefreelibrary.com/Elijah+and+Elisha%3A+part+II+similarities+and+differences.-a0312508430
[90] Ibid
[91] Ibid.
[92] https://www.inc.com/peter-economy/3-surprising-things-you-didn-t-know-about-millennials.html
[93] https://www.hrdive.com/news/the-millennial-edge-how-to-use-this-generation-as-a-competitive-advantage/507495/
[94] Ray Stedman, Talking to My Father, Barbour & Co, 1997.
[95] https://www.addeigloriam.org/stories/morrison.htm
[96] http://www.missionarycare.com/about-reentry-2.html

[97] https://www.mayoclinic.org/diseases-conditions/agoraphobia/symptoms-causes/syc-20355987

www.ingramcontent.com/pod-product-compliance
Lightning Source LLC
LaVergne TN
LVHW051547070426
835507LV00021B/2442